DATE DUE

5'03			

DEMCO 38-296

When Officials Clash

When Officials Clash

◆ ◆

Implementation of the Civil Rights of Institutionalized Persons Act

Karen E. Holt

PRAEGER

Westport, Connecticut
London

Library of Congress Cataloging-in-Publication Data

Holt, Karen E., 1955–
    When officials clash : implementation of the Civil Rights of
Institutionalized Persons Act / Karen E. Holt.
       p.   cm.
    Includes bibliographical references (p.   ) and index.
    ISBN 0–275–95997–X (alk. paper)
    1. Mental health laws—United States.   2. Insane—Commitment and
detention—United States.   3. Inmates of institutions—Civil rights—
United States.   4. Bureaucracy—United States.   5. United States.
Civil Rights of Institutionalized Persons Act.   I. Title.
KF3828.H65   1998
344.73′044—dc21   97–27922

British Library Cataloguing in Publication Data is available.

Library of Congress Catalog Card Number: 97–27922
ISBN: 0–275–95997–X

First published in 1998

Praeger Publishers, 88 Post Road West, Westport, CT 06881
An imprint of Greenwood Publishing Group, Inc.

Printed in the United States of America

The paper used in this book complies with the
Permanent Paper Standard issued by the National
Information Standards Organization (Z39.48–1984).

10 9 8 7 6 5 4 3 2 1

To John Gittleman and J. E. Holt

The greatest men I will ever know.

Contents

Preface

From August 1983 until September 1984, I worked as an attorney in the Special Litigation Section of the Civil Rights Division of the Department of Justice, my first job as a young attorney just out of law school. At the time I arrived, the Section was in the midst of a maelstrom of controversy between careerists within the agency who strongly advocated vigorous enforcement of civil rights law, and political appointees bent on curtailing the Department's historical level of activity. Conflict was rampant and departures frequent. At the end of my one-year tenure, I had been in the Section longer than all but four of the line attorneys still remaining.

This research is an effort to examine the activities of that time, as well as to shed light on the management style of the Reagan Administration, at least with respect to appointees like William Bradford Reynolds who remained committed throughout the Administration to the fundamental principles upon which Reaganism was founded. It is meant to neither praise nor indict, but rather to provide an analytical framework for understanding the lessons of that time and for applying those lessons in the future.

I was inspired to pursue this project by the thankless work of many Justice Department attorneys. My efforts would have been far less substantive without the assistance of the attorneys who contributed their time, particularly Arthur Peabody, Robert Dinerstein, Robinsue Frohboese, and John MacCoon. Their inspiring dedication gives hope to those who depend upon the unrecognized and unrewarded work of civil servants. My doctoral advisor, Dr. Michael R. Fitzgerald, and committee, Lawrence Dessem, Dr. Patricia Freeland, Dr. Lilliard Richardson, and particularly Dr. Otis Stephens, Jr., deserve thanks for their untiring pursuit of excellence. Dr. Bill Lyons, Dr. Robert Maranto, and Dr. Grant Neeley assisted with the CRIPA survey, but they bear no responsibility for any shortcomings. Insightful comments on research in progress were made by Dr. Robert Durant and Dr. William Blomquist, and Hofstra University's excellent conference on the Reagan Presidency led to important contacts for this research. On a personal level, long days of lonely writing were made more tolerable by the companionship of my Labrador retriever, Georgia, and the interruptions she forced. Finally and most importantly, I thank my husband, Dr. John Gittleman, who lovingly combines the roles of advisor, supporter, tactician, and friend.

• 1 •

Change and Conflict

Much has been written of the bitter confrontations between Reagan Administration political appointees and civil servants, particularly in areas such as environmental and civil rights policies where the Administration sought to redirect the enforcement activities of federal agencies. Analysts have used images of colliding worlds and seismic upheavals to depict the clashes, similar in nature to those occurring during prior instances of policy redirection, though sometimes differing in publicity and magnitude. This book concerns such a confrontation, one especially notable for the lengthy tenure of the political appointee involved and the extent to which career employees opposed him. From this examination come lessons about the roles of each party in the policy process, the impact of other actors such as Congress and stakeholders, and the long-term effect of administrative control of the bureaucracy.

Ronald Reagan's eventful two-term administration invigorated study of the institution of the presidency. Theories of presidential management and policy success could be analyzed using data accumulated over a longer period of time than had been possible for several prior administrations, and the Reagan approach to governing spawned analyses by participants, proponents, and critics. Research on the administrative presidency benefited greatly from the Reagan years. The term "administrative presidency," attributed to Nathan (1983a), refers to the pursuit of presidential policy goals through strategic management of the bureaucracy, rather than by seeking or amending legislation. Prior to Ronald Reagan, the most visible user of the strategy was Richard Nixon (Aberbach & Rockman, 1990; Nathan, 1983a). That prototype for the application of an administrative strategy provided mixed support for the belief that the strategy could be followed successfully. In the case of Ronald Reagan, however, there is general consensus that he succeeded in achieving his policy preferences using an administrative strategy, although the same tactics contributing to that success arguably led to the greatest failure of the Reagan presidency—the Iran-contra affair (Anderson, 1990; Henderson, 1988).

This book focuses on one activity of the Reagan Administration—the implementation of a particular civil rights statute—to examine in detail the conditions under which an administrative strategy is most likely to fulfill presidential policy goals. It synthesizes research in public administration, specifically in implementation studies and examinations of careerist/political appointee relations, with research on the presidency. This synthesis across fields is essential to fully assess the effect of an administrative strategy.

Proponents of the strategy contend that it enhances democratic values because it promotes the responsiveness of the bureaucracy to the electorate. Critics, however, point out that continuity and consistency within the bureaucracy are important to ensure bureaucratic performance, as well as providing a check on excessive ideological or partisan fervor on the part of elected officials. Although bureaucrats are expected to accede to political direction, they often educate political appointees about the danger and impracticality of rapid change, and may even actively obstruct change. They are said to evince "loyalty that argues back" (Heclo, 1975, p. 82). The impact of an administrative strategy on careerists is a critical but largely overlooked factor affecting the success of an administrative strategy, and is also important in addressing the larger issue of the implications of an administrative approach to governance.

This focus of this book is the Reagan Administration's use of an administrative strategy in implementing the Civil Rights of Institutionalized Persons Act (CRIPA), a law signed by President Jimmy Carter on May 23, 1980. CRIPA gives the Attorney General standing to file suits against states allegedly maintaining unconstitutional conditions of confinement within state institutions, such as prisons, facilities for the mentally retarded, and hospitals for the mentally ill.

Although the passage of CRIPA clarified the Attorney General's authority to file suit, the Justice Department had been actively involved in landmark institutional litigation of the 1970s, and CRIPA was expected to facilitate that continued involvement. Proposed initially during the Ford Administration, the primary impetus for CRIPA came from the Carter Justice Department, which had two lawsuits challenging institutional conditions dismissed because there was no statute specifically giving standing to the Attorney General. There was virtually no implementation of CRIPA during the Carter Administration, due to the late date of the law's enactment and the time periods it contained for promulgating regulations and notifying targeted states prior to formally initiating investigations. The basis for CRIPA, federal involvement in the internal activities of states, was anathema to the federalism and deregulatory preferences of the incoming Reagan Administration.

Rather than seeking to amend or repeal CRIPA, the Administration adopted an administrative strategy of limited enforcement, which became a deliberate and even open preference of the Reagan Administration. Congress, despite having recently enacted the law, for various reasons did little to alter the course of enforcement. The greatest opposition faced by the Administration in pursuing its policy preference toward CRIPA came from career employees in the enforcing section of the Department of Justice, many of whom had eagerly anticipated the day when the enabling legislation would finally pass. This combination of factors—a statute with no history of enforcement, an ideologically hostile administration, an ambivalent Congress, and vocal careerists, make the administrative implementation of CRIPA a unique opportunity to observe the pursuit of a policy preference through the use of an administrative strategy.

ADMINISTRATIVE STRATEGY

The Reagan presidency is especially appropriate for a study linking factors relevant to implementation success and the use of an administrative strategy. As noted by Palumbo and Calista (1990), "The Reagan Administration seems to have understood the political nature of implementation better than previous administrations. It sought to redirect many policies through implementation rather than by seeking new legislation, which it knew it could not get" (p. 7). Although implementation of any statute necessarily means implementation of the president's policy preference with respect to that statute, the manner in which a president seeks to achieve his preferred policy can vary. Use of an administrative strategy is supported by those who favor increased executive leadership (Eastland, 1992), and criticized by those who do not equate presidential strength with better government (Kraft & Vig, 1984).

In his seminal book on presidential power, Richard Neustadt (1980) stated that the office of the president is weak, not powerful, due primarily to the fact that government is structured so as to make the president but one of many actors in the political process. Given what Neustadt viewed as the inherent weaknesses of the office, a president, to be successful, must rely on personal attributes such as bargaining skills, reputation, and prestige. Even in a later edition assessing the Reagan years, Neustadt did not retreat from this theme of weakness, stating that Reagan had "left behind a glow of temporary mastery" of the office (Neustadt, 1990, p. x).

A president who chooses to manage actively and to look for sources of presidential power can turn the office weakness perceived by Neustadt into an office strength (Eastland, 1992). One way a president can increase his influence is to exercise better the power he has to administratively select and manage appointees. Nathan (1983a) termed the use of this active management role the "administrative presidency" strategy, defined as the concept that policy objectives can best be carried out by administrative action, "that is, by using the discretion permitted in the implementation of new laws rather than advancing these policy aims through the enactment of new legislation" (Nathan, 1983a, p. 7). Nathan describes how President Nixon moved from the legislative emphasis of his first term to an administrative approach that ultimately proved unsuccessful in the aftermath of Watergate. In Ronald Reagan's presidency, Nathan found a successful example of the use of the administrative strategy. Nathan gives Reagan high marks, and emphasizes that it would be appropriate for liberals to adopt a similar approach should they have the opportunity (Nathan, 1984). In comparison to President Nixon, however, Reagan had the advantage of several factors that made success of an administrative strategy more likely: his electoral margin was larger; he initially had a Republican Senate; he selected his own subcabinet; and the civil service was more susceptible to political influence due to the 1978 passage of the Civil Service Reform Act (Aberbach, Rockman, & Copeland, 1990).

By actively seeking to manage the bureaucracy, a president can promote his own policy preferences within the administrative framework, rather than the more cumbersome means of proposing and enacting new legislation or amending existing law. The administrative strategy has been criticized for being ineffective in achieving the policy preferences of the executive, and as an unnecessarily confrontational and inappropriate use of presidential power (Waterman, 1989). But Nathan contends that Reagan was effective in achieving his policy goals, and that the strategy is a legitimate and essential tool to further national policy preferences: "A managerial emphasis on the part of the president enhances popular control, given the tendency of industrialized states to become increasingly controlled from bureaucratic and technocratic power centers. The exercise of a greater measure of civilian control over the executive branch of the American national government, properly reflective of legal and constitutional requirements, is fully consistent with democratic values" (Nathan, 1983a, p. 83). By "democratic values," Nathan primarily refers to the government's "ability to respond to changes in basic social values" (p. 12).

Newland (1983) examined what he called the "ideological political administration" of Reagan's first term, a phrase he used to describe Reagan's administrative management style. Newland raised concerns about whether Reagan's management approach relied too heavily on ideological and partisan considerations, and whether "Reaganism is a revolutionary break with all of America's distinctive political traditions" (p. 20). The contrast between Nathan's view that an administrative strategy is consistent with democratic values, and Newland's that it is a break with America's political traditions, echoes the long-standing debate about the proper role of politics in administration.

An empirical examination of Reagan's administrative strategy was made by Durant (1987, 1992) in a review of environmental policy in the Bureau of Land Management's (BLM) management of New Mexico sites. Durant concluded that the problems he observed in the BLM situation indicate flaws in the application of the administrative strategy, not in the administrative presidency approach per se, and identifies conditions that affect the levels of conflict produced by an administrative strategy.

Critics of the strategy, perhaps partially due to disagreement with the policy preferences of presidents who have most assiduously pursued an administrative strategy (Mann, 1990), charge that Nathan and others overstate the capability and desirability of a president to influence administrative actions. Waterman (1989) discusses four instances that he contends illustrate that the success, if any, of a presidential administrative strategy is limited and short-lived. His criticism of the confrontational nature of the administrative presidency strategy includes conclusions drawn from four case studies, two from the Reagan years. Waterman suggests that presidents should learn to recognize the factors that increase the likelihood of success of the strategy, and refrain from using it when those factors are not present. He views the administrative strategy as inherently confrontational, and believes that any short-term gains that might be realized by such a strategy are likely to result in modifying legislation or some other backlash, leading to a diminution of presidential power. In Waterman's opinion, the primary value of the administrative strategy is in the identification of certain tools that can enhance the likelihood of success of a different strategy, one that includes consultation with Congress. Waterman, however, prefers and recommends a presidential strategy of cooperation, not consultation, which he predicts will be more successful in achieving the policy that the president prefers.

CAREERIST-POLITICAL APPOINTEE RELATIONS

Neutral v. Responsive Competence

Few today subscribe to the old politics/administration dichotomy, or the "hopelessly naive" notion that political considerations do not play a role in administrative decisions (Pfiffner, 1991, p. 72). Although there is general agreement that the dichotomy does not exist, it is less easy to reach a consensus on the extent to which politics should be a part of administration. "The issue here is not politicization, but *undue* politicization" (Huddleston, 1987, p. 58). In many ways, this is also the main issue in the ongoing debate about the value of an administrative strategy—determining when it is appropriate as well as when it works.

Before the term administrative presidency was popularized, those concerned with executive leadership recognized the conflict inherent in expecting civil servants to respond to executive policy direction, while also applying their professional expertise. The dilemma was framed as being between two types of competence, *responsive*, or "the extent to which outputs from a bureaucracy change with application of an external political stimulus" (Wood & Waterman, 1991, p. 825), versus *neutral*, which emphasizes the skill and experience of professionals in making policy decisions. The problem was thought to be how to achieve balance between the two, rather than whether or how to elevate one over the other (Kaufman, 1956).

A fundamental problem in using a neutral/responsive competence framework is that it equates expertise with neutrality, ignoring how that expertise is acquired and developed. "Most agency officials and scientists involved in policy disputes for any significant length of time are not neutral but instead are members of advocacy coalitions" (Sabatier & Zafonte, 1994, p. 2). In attempting to reach a conclusion about the respective roles of neutral versus responsive competence in civil servants, the politics/administration dichotomy debate resurfaces, just as it does in discussions about an administrative strategy. Sabatier and Zafonte attempt to avoid this dilemma by redefining neutral competence as "the absence of—or at least the refusal to act on the basis of—personal obligations; a commitment to be guided solely by the instructions of hierarchical superiors" (p. 2), a definition resembling *responsive* competence. The difficulty in defining the elements of responsive and neutral competence, as well as in determining the appropriate bounds of each, is a long-recognized problem. "Political scientists of the remoter future, looking back, may well conclude that it is not easy to bridge the gap between a generation seeking to encourage the growth of a professional bureaucracy and a generation in turmoil over how to control it" (Kaufman, 1956, p. 1073).

Kaufman's "remoter future" has arrived, as shown by criticism of the use of an administrative strategy (Waterman, 1989), as well as by the volume of research examining the relationship between political appointees and career employees. There is talk of the need to reach an understanding (Nathan, 1986), a balance (Ban & Ingraham, 1990), and an equilibrium (Aberbach, Rockman & Copeland, 1990), in the relationship between political appointees and career employees.

Where there is a sharp contrast in the goals of political appointees and the attitudes of careerists, such as that which occurred in many policy areas during the Reagan Administration, conflict is inevitable (Aberbach & Rockman,

1990; Durant, 1990). The effect of the clash between political appointees and careerists can influence the outcome of an administrative strategy. Some believe the conflict will always be detrimental: "When two worlds collide, the president's program can only suffer—unless, of course, conflict and disruption are part of the agenda" (Light, 1987, p. 156). On the other hand, the optimal use of an administrative strategy would seek to minimize the adverse effects of the dispute. Understanding the options available to careerists disagreeing with executive policy direction can inform ways to limit the detrimental effects careerist reaction may cause.

Careerist Response to Administrative Direction

Nathan (1986) recognized that one effect of an administrative strategy is a decline in the morale of career employees. Where there is a redirection of implementation or a pronounced shift in policy emphasis, career employees who had worked under previous administrations may feel betrayed and disillusioned. Although Heclo observed that the price of job security for civil servants should be a willing responsiveness to legitimate political leaders, he noted that "political figures who hope to lead Washington's bureaucracies face the fundamental problem of trying to generate the changes they want without losing the bureaucratic services they need" (Heclo, 1977, p. 235).

A highly visible or protracted conflict between careerists and political appointees committed to carrying out administrative policies can thwart the success of an administrative strategy, especially one that pursues only limited implementation of a law. "Those attracted to work for government agencies are likely to support the policies [historically] carried out by those agencies" (Edwards, 1980, p. 90), policies that new political appointees may not always wish to continue. Careerists who worked under prior administrations with differing policy preferences tend to accept those earlier priorities as the mission of the agencies, becoming "past majorities against the wishes of specific (executive) Administrations that seek to alter those priorities through political appointments" (Sabatier & Zafonte, 1994, p. 4). Appointees may lack sensitivity to or concern about the effects of their actions on civil servants (Heclo, 1987), often having as their primary concern the president's reelection or setting the stage for a favored successor (Pfiffner, 1988). Although low morale can lead to a mass exodus of employees and therefore presumably less opposition within the agency, it can also result in more attention from outside parties such as Congress and the media, leading to increased confrontation and a decrease in the likelihood that the administrative policy will succeed (Durant, 1992).

Research in this area has examined the choices available to careerists who disagree with a new or shifted policy, drawing explicitly and implicitly upon the "exit, voice, and loyalty" model (Hirschman, 1970). Careerists may try to change a policy with which they disagree, and if unsuccessful, stay and accept the new policy or leave, usually seeking to leave if their disagreement is strong and the likelihood of change slight (Schmidt & Abramson, 1983). Those who care most may leave first (Hirschman, 1970). Actions may be variations of Hirschman's model. For example, those who stay may not be loyal, and may perform their duties half-heartedly as a sort of benign neglect (Lowery & Rusbelt, 1986). They may devise ways to limit the damage of policies they dislike (Campbell, 1986), and can even engage in active sabotage, at least from the perspective of the political appointees (Heritage Foundation, 1984).

When careerists view the position taken by appointees as inimicable to the central mission of the agency, they are likely to use their strongest efforts to oppose the administrative action (Durant, 1992), leading to hostility and nonnegotiable demands by careerists. Schmidt & Abramson (1983) term agencies experiencing such conflict "lost," and they find that the ensuing turmoil often results in the departure of the best persons and the inability to recruit qualified replacements. Nathan sees the impact of an administrative strategy on careerists as perhaps its greatest drawback:

The principal issue I raise is the effect of this kind of administrative strategy on the character and morale of the career service. Values associated with the importance of the role of professional employees in the career service are juxtaposed with arguments in support of an administrative strategy for political executives; the trade-off is one between the political process and professional expertise. No definite conclusion can be reached on this issue. Career officials perceive themselves as being threatened (and they are threatened) by the approach described here. This perceived threat not only has a negative impact on the existing staff—weakening morale and in some cases causing early exits of capable career officials—but it also tends to have a dampening effect on the recruitment of new government employees. (1986, p. 132)

By characterizing the dilemma created by an administrative strategy as a trade-off between the political process and professional expertise, Nathan does not acknowledge the political considerations underlying the expertise of careerists. But careerists see their duty as multifaceted: obviously to the chief executive, but also to what they perceive to be the legislative intent, the public interest, the agency's clientele, current members of Congress, and even to each other. When careerists view these obligations as divergent, particularly in periods of divided government, opposition to political direction is likely to be strong and administrative efforts at control pronounced (Aberbach & Rockman, 1990).

Many concerns have been raised about the long-term effect of this tension on the agency. Widespread departure of careerists may lead to a "hemorrhaging of excellence" (Kirschten, 1983, p. 732), a decline in the ability to attract good people to work in government (Goldstein, 1992), and the eventual erosion of the capacity of the workforce (Benda & Levine, 1988; Moe, 1985). Even without the widespread departure of careerists, an agency can suffer from careerist-appointee tension. Careerists are hesitant to speak openly (Huddleston, 1987; Landsberg, 1993), and conflicts emerge. The agency does whatever it is going to do with less efficiency and more distrust (Landsberg, 1993). Changes that could assist the administration may not come about because careerists fear to speak, and appointees are wary of encouraging dialogue. Each group shuts itself out from the influence of the other (Landsberg, 1993), avoiding discussion that could "season and temper" the necessary process of achieving a larger public good (Ingraham & Ban, 1988). Those affected by policy do not know how to proceed, because they see inconsistency and uncertainty (Landsberg, 1993).

Although the link between an administrative strategy and deleterious effects on careerists is difficult to establish and vulnerable to subjective interpretation (Durant, 1992, p. xii), the impact on career civil servants and how that affects the operation of the agency are important components in assessing the effectiveness of an administrative strategy. Unless the executive's goal is to totally dismantle the agency rather than merely limit, redirect, or rein in its activities, it is in the executive's interest to ensure the retention of at least a small cadre of experienced careerists, to take advantage of their institutional knowledge and experience (Campbell, 1986). Perhaps of more relevance to the success of an administrative strategy, open hostility from careerists and noisy departures increase the likelihood of third-party involvement, which could seriously threaten the pursuit of administrative policy preferences. Additionally, in terms of the willingness of careerists to accede to a change in administrative direction, it is preferable for any policy change to be incremental. Retention of some careerists in order to retain institutional knowledge and expertise may be critical to an incremental process.

Democratic Values

One reason Nathan cites in favor of a president's use of an administrative strategy is that it allows the government to better reflect the will of the people, promoting the democratic value of political responsiveness. In our government, the people's will is manifested through the election of representatives, who are then expected to make decisions in a manner that comports with that will. Under this view, the president has a right and an obligation to use the management tool of personnel administration (Huddleston, 1987). If the executive is not reflecting the will of the people, he faces election defeat or correction by the people's other representative, Congress.

In assessing the reaction of careerists to administrative direction and the overall effect of the use of such a strategy, political responsiveness is not the only democratic value, and the President and Congress are not the only actors in the policy process. Particularly when civil rights are at stake, protection of minority interests is another democratic value that can be affected by the use of an administrative strategy, and the judiciary has played a critical role in ensuring the protection of minority rights.

Those who believe careerists should provide responsive competence at the direction of political appointees contend that it is more consistent with the democratic value "that only elected officials or those whom they select to act on their behalf are to make policy" (Aberbach & Rockman, 1990, p. 41). Neutral competence proponents view the democratic system as being designed to create checks on political zeal and rapid change, and the moderating influence of the bureaucracy protects the long-term interest of the electorate. The bureaucracy thus should operate as a moderating influence because there is often no specific mandate from the people on particular issues (Shanley, 1992), and Congress for various reasons rarely engages in the type of oversight that would check the executive branch's actions (Mezey, 1989). Executive actions that unduly infringe minority rights might not trigger public or legislative concern (Leadership Conference, 1983), and some groups may lack effective access to the courts. Because an administrative strategy seems to favor responsive competence over neutral, Rourke (1992) poses a question to consider in evaluating the impact of an administrative strategy: "Is there a fundamental element that government bureaucrats bring to the process through which public policy is made in the United States that it would otherwise lack, and even more important, that it cannot do without?" (p. 539). Rourke concludes that the bureaucrats' informed criticism . . . will help anticipate and avert problems that may arise when the [administration's] decisions are put into effect" (p. 545). More significantly, careerist response may help protect minority rights.

The application and success of the administrative presidency strategy depends on the circumstances surrounding the policy involved and the skill of the actor, just as these factors have been linked to implementation success or failure. Additionally, the response of careerists affects the success of the administrative strategy, as well as the impact the strategy has on democratic values such as public responsiveness and protection of minority rights. Research in these areas forms the basis for the theoretical framework for this study, which is described in Appendix A.

CRIPA is a textbook example of the use of an administrative strategy in the face of careerist resistance. To understand how the clash developed, the foundations of CRIPA, including its legislative history and major provisions, are detailed in the next chapter. In Chapter 3, the Reagan ideology in general and policy preference toward CRIPA in particular are examined. Chapter 4 discusses the enforcement of CRIPA by the Reagan Administration. Chapters 5 and 6 review the response to CRIPA enforcement from those outside of the Department of Justice, primarily Congress and stakeholders, and the effect of CRIPA enforcement on the careerists within the Department of Justice and the actions they took in response to that enforcement.

An administrative strategy has effects that extend far past the administration that employs it, and these are examined in the remaining chapters. The factors affecting the outcome of the Reagan Administration's implementation of CRIPA are discussed in Chapter 7. Ultimately, a determination of the usefulness of an administrative strategy must consider what happens in its wake, and how that may alter an assessment of when and to what extent it should be used. This text therefore concludes with an evaluation of the administrative strategy's impact on democratic governance.

◆ 2 ◆

The Evolution of CRIPA

"One measure of a nation's civilization is the quality of treatment it provides persons entrusted to its care" (H.R. Rep. No. 897, 1980 p. 8).

Most persons never see the inside of a prison or state hospital, and become aware of conditions only generally, if at all, when they see a documentary or read about a well-publicized lawsuit. Institutional conditions receive little attention in large part because of the nature of the population affected, most of whom are unable to express their feelings or command attention due to their disability or illness, or for prisoners, because they do not engender sympathy due to the acts that led to their incarceration. The hidden nature of institutional problems, the inability of the population to get assistance on its own behalf, and stiff competition for scarce state resources, historically have made the federal government the primary actor in litigation to redress unacceptable conditions within state institutions.

THE DEPARTMENT OF JUSTICE AND INSTITUTIONAL LITIGATION

Prior to the Reagan Administration, the litigating sections of the Civil Rights Division of the Department of Justice were given great discretion in their operations. That discretion was generally used to advocate vigorously on behalf of persons protected by the civil rights statutes the Division enforced. Even before the introduction of the legislation that eventually became CRIPA, the Civil Rights Division for many years had engaged in complex litigation addressing conditions in state-run institutions such as prisons, mental retardation facilities, and hospitals for the mentally ill. The Justice Department's participation contributed to landmark judicial decisions in this area, including those involving conditions in Alabama mental institutions (*Wyatt v. Stickney*, 1971); the Willowbrook State School for the Mentally Retarded in New York (*New York State Association for Retarded Children v. Rockefeller*, 1975); the Pennhurst State School and Hospital in Pennsylvania (*Halderman v. Pennhurst State School and Hospital*, 1977); and the Oklahoma and Texas prison systems (*Battle v. Anderson*, 1977; *Ruiz v. Estelle*, 1982). Although these lawsuits were not initiated by the federal government, the Justice Department took an active role on behalf of the plaintiffs in all of the cases, either as a plaintiff-intervenor or as *amicus curiae* (literally friend of the court, but more accurately friend of the plaintiff in these instances).

The *Wyatt* and Willowbrook lawsuits illustrate the type of lawsuits that were brought to secure fundamental rights for institutionalized individuals, and the role of the Justice Department in the litigation. The *Wyatt* case was initially filed by guardians of patients at Alabama's Bryce Hospital for the Mentally Ill. The presiding judge in that case, Frank M. Johnson, Jr., requested the Attorney General to appear on behalf of the United States as litigating *amicus curiae*, and to assist the court by presenting evidence of institutional conditions, evaluating the adequacy of the hospital's treatment programs, and assisting state officials in their efforts to meet federal standards for adequate care. Judge Johnson took notice at the conclusion of the trial of the exemplary service provided by the Department of Justice. The Department also served as litigating *amicus* in the Willowbrook case.

Because its role in such litigation was confined to being intervenor or *amicus curiae*, the Justice Department could be involved only in cases filed by others, meaning that there had to be a plaintiff with standing and enough resources to commence the lawsuit. To try to broaden its oversight to include institutions for which there were no individuals or advocacy groups involved in litigation, the Department of Justice initiated some lawsuits in its own name. This action was taken despite the fact that the Attorney General did not have the express statutory authority to initiate or intervene in litigation seeking redress for alleged violations of the constitutional rights of institutionalized persons. The Department of Justice contended that it had inherent authority to challenge unconstitutional conditions, but the lack of clear statutory authorization cast doubt on the Justice Department's power to initiate lawsuits where no other parties were involved, or even to compel the grant of its request for intervention in the face of a judge unwilling to do so.

In *United States v. Solomon* (1976, 1977), the Attorney General filed suit to enjoin the practices and policies of Maryland officials who administered Rosewood State Hospital, the state's major facility for the mentally retarded. The defendants filed a motion to dismiss on the ground that the Attorney General lacked standing to bring the suit. The Attorneys General of Pennsylvania (site of Pennhurst State Hospital, another likely federal target) and Texas (already a battleground over its prison system), filed *amici* briefs in support of dismissal. The district court granted Maryland's motion to dismiss, basing its decision on "the premise that the executive branch has no power and therefore no legal standing to bring this suit unless such authority can be found, either explicitly or implicitly, in the scheme of government laid out by the Constitution" (*United States v. Solomon*, 1976, p. 362). The court concluded that principles of federalism required that the action be dismissed in the absence of express statutory authority to sue granted by Congress to the Attorney General. The circuit court affirmed, stressing that the doctrine of separation of powers compelled the result; to do otherwise would be tantamount to permitting the executive branch to legislate. The reasoning of *Solomon* was adopted by both the district and circuit courts in *United States v. Mattson* (1979), a suit to address conditions in a Montana facility for the mentally retarded. The same issues were also raised in cases involving a Puerto Rican juvenile facility and a detention facility in Cook County, Illinois.

The Department of Justice accepted the *Solomon* court's implied invitation to seek legislative action, and the holdings in *Solomon* and *Mattson* provided the impetus for the passage of CRIPA. The Senate Report accompanying CRIPA stated that "the Attorney General's dependence on the selection of litigation by private parties constitutes a barrier to the most efficient and effective utilization of the Justice Department's resources" (S. Rep. No. 416, 1979, p. 16).

PROVISIONS OF CRIPA

The primary purpose of CRIPA is to give the Attorney General standing to initiate or intervene in lawsuits addressing institutional conditions, but its other provisions provide detailed procedures for the exercise of that authority. The text of CRIPA is summarized briefly below.

CRIPA consists of eleven sections. The first broadly defines institution. The next provides that the Attorney General may bring an action against any state, political subdivision, or official, when the Attorney General has reasonable cause to believe that institutionalized persons are being subjected to egregious or flagrant conditions, which deprive such persons of any rights, privileges, or immunities secured or protected by the constitution or laws of the United

States; that such persons are thereby suffering grievous harm; and that such deprivation is pursuant to a pattern or practice. The relief that may be ordered is the equitable relief necessary to ensure minimum corrective measures.

The Attorney General can commence an investigation into conditions at an institution only after at least seven days' notice. Further, prior to filing a lawsuit, the Attorney General must certify that at least 49 days previously a letter was sent to the state's Governor and Attorney General notifying them of the allegations, their factual bases, and the minimal corrective measures required to remedy them. The Attorney General must also certify that an effort has been made to consult state officials, that the Attorney General has unsuccessfully attempted to resolve the matter informally, and that sufficient time has passed for remedial action to have been taken. Similar requirements apply to intervention in an ongoing case, except that at least 90 days must have passed between the commencement of the action and the filing of a motion to intervene.

Much of the legislative debate over CRIPA concerned the extent to which it should apply to prison conditions. CRIPA provides that suits may be filed to redress prison conditions only if such conditions allegedly deprive prisoners of *constitutional* rights, not federal statutory rights. The Attorney General was given the authority to promulgate minimum standards for the resolution of inmate grievances, or the Attorney General could choose to review a state's own promulgation of standards. Although the creation of such standards could be viewed as an expansion of the Attorney General's regulatory authority, the real purpose of this provision was to limit prisoner litigation, for prisoners would have to exhaust all of their administrative remedies under such standards before they could file their own actions under 42 U.S.C. Section 1983 (1981).

Most of CRIPA's provisions were drawn from existing civil rights legislation. For example, the authority granted to the Attorney General to initiate litigation when the Attorney General has reason to believe there is a pattern or practice of depriving persons of rights secured by the Constitution and federal law is similar to the power given the Attorney General under Title VI of the Civil Rights Act of 1960 (voting discrimination); titles II and VII of the Civil Rights Act of 1964 (public accommodation and employment discrimination); title VIII of the Civil Rights Act of 1968 (housing discrimination); and section 122 (c) of the State and Local Fiscal Assistance Act of 1972 (discrimination in programs receiving federal assistance). The Senate Report on CRIPA indicates that the descriptive terms "pattern or practice" and "egregious or flagrant conditions . . . causing . . . grievous harm" are "intended to parallel the limitations that have been applied to actions brought under 42 U.S.C. Section 1983 and similar rights enforcement statutes" (S. Rep. No. 416, 1979, p. 29). The authorization given to the Attorney General to "seek such equitable relief as may be appropriate" to ensure the full enjoyment of any rights, privileges, or immunities secured by the Constitution and federal law is similar to that contained in various titles of the Civil Rights Act of 1964 and Title VIII of the Civil Rights Act of 1968.

The primary provisions of CRIPA were thus meant to have meanings already established in law and precedent, and that history was cited to address concerns raised during the CRIPA hearings about the scope of enforcement activity that Congress was being asked to authorize (S. Rep. No. 416, 1979, pp. 39–42). The statutes that served as the sources for the language defining the scope of the Department of Justice's authority under CRIPA, however, did not contain the limits on the exercise of that authority which were included in CRIPA. The ambiguity of legislative intent regarding CRIPA, evidenced by statutory limitations and procedural protections not present in preceding civil rights legislation, placed the responsibility for making choices about CRIPA's enforcement squarely on the executive branch (Percy, 1989, p. 254).

LEGISLATIVE HISTORY OF CRIPA

The bill that became CRIPA originated in the Senate as S. 1393, and was introduced by Senator Birch Bayh (D-Ind.) on April 26, 1977. Although Senator Bayh contended that his staff was responsible for drafting the bill, it is clear from the Justice Department's participation at every stage of the debate that it was closely involved in promoting the bill, if not the actual drafter. S. 1393, and its House counterpart, H.R. 9400, never reached the floor of their respective houses due to delaying tactics on the part of Thomas Kindness (R-Oh.) in the House and filibuster threats in the Senate, primarily by Robert Morgan (D-N.C.) and Strom Thurmond (R-S.C.), all of whom opposed the enlargement of federal intervention in state matters.

In 1979, S. 10, a bill similar to H.R. 9400, was introduced in the Senate by a bipartisan group of 22 senators. Extensive hearings on H.R. 9400 and S. 10 were conducted in 1977 and 1979, with proponents presenting horror stories of abuses and tragedies in institutions, in contrast to the predictions of infringement on states' rights and descriptions of past abuses of authority by the Justice Department detailed by opponents. The National Association of (State) Attorneys General was the most vigorous and outspoken opponent of the legislation, with the possible exception of witnesses presented by Senators James Exon (D-Neb.), John Danforth (R-Mo.), and Thurmond, who described what they viewed as strong-arm tactics by the Justice Department in the course of institutional litigation in their states.

A great deal of the debate and modification of S. 10 concerned mechanisms to mitigate the enforcement power of the Department of Justice, and the frequency with which that power would be used. In response to these concerns, in testimony on the Senate floor, Senator Bayh listed ten safeguards that had been inserted in the bill to provide for review by the Justice Department before lawsuits could be filed: a 55-day notice requirement before a lawsuit could be filed (later shortened to 49); providing a statement of underlying facts in the notice letter; requiring the Attorney General to state minimal corrective measures; listing proposed remedies as precisely as possible; notifying the state of any available federal assistance; discussing the cost of the remedial action; giving the state the opportunity to informally and voluntarily correct the deficiency; and requiring the Attorney General to personally certify the action, the complaint, and the facts contained within the complaint (126 Cong. Rec. S1712–13).

Lynn Walker Huntley, a Deputy Assistant Attorney General during the CRIPA debate, explained that while she and other proponents would have preferred not to have included all of these procedural requirements, reality dictated that certain compromises had to be made: "The choice was, shall we concede the language or shall we have no statute at all" (Interview with Lynn Walker Huntley, 1995). Ms. Huntley went on to say, however, that proponents recognized that the procedural requirements could actually benefit Departmental enforcement activity, for by having specific procedural markers the Department would be less vulnerable to criticism of overzealousness in its enforcement.

Attorney General Griffin Bell and Drew Days, Assistant Attorney General for Civil Rights, testified at various times that they anticipated that the Justice Department would continue the same litigation pace under CRIPA as it previously had maintained for institutional lawsuits. Further, to ensure that the actions of the Department of Justice could be subject to informed congressional review, CRIPA imposed an obligation on the Attorney General to annually report to Congress on the number or variety and outcome of all actions instituted, to detail the procedures involved in each case, to analyze the impact of the actions including an estimate of the cost incurred by states to defend, to state the assistance made available by the federal government to help states correct problems, as well as to state the progress made in federal institutions toward meeting promulgated standards for conditions therein. Various congressional subcommittees, including those charged with oversight of the conditions of the handicapped, were expected to be involved in monitoring the actions of the Department of Justice.

The final version of CRIPA bore little resemblance to the broad grants of administrative authority that characterized earlier civil rights laws, even though much of its text had been drawn from prior legislation. Although the accounts of institutional horror during the hearing were so graphic and troubling that they engendered bipartisan support for CRIPA, the anecdotes of prosecutorial and investigatory abuse by the Department of Justice resulted in the inclusion of significant checks on the Department's exercise of its newly-granted authority. Additionally, Congress placed a great deal of oversight responsibility on the Attorney General, who was charged with personally certifying that procedural safeguards had been satisfied prior to instituting litigation. This personal certification would enable an executive appointee to act as a curb on the presumed zeal of career Justice attorneys, in effect amounting to legislatively sanctioning or at least acquiescing in the use of an administrative strategy in CRIPA implementation. When coupled with legislative silence on the conditions that should be redressed, Congress gave the Department of Justice great discretion to interpret CRIPA.

The legislative compromises necessary to pass CRIPA facilitated an administrative strategy of limited enforcement. Structure and process requirements in a law "build delay and bias into administrative procedures" (Hill & Brazier, 1991, p. 375). The greatest specificity in CRIPA was in the passages constraining the federal government's ability to enforce it. The vagueness of statutory language concerning conditions and remedies effected a transfer of ultimate policy decisionmaking to the implementing agency. Legislative vagueness such as that present in CRIPA was necessary in order to build a favorable voting coalition (Aberbach & Rockman, 1993), but it is not necessarily a reflection of legislative goals (Wood et al., 1993). Congress simply did not address specifically conditions to be redressed and remedies to be imposed, in effect passively approving executive management and control (Aman, 1992). Given the historic advocacy role of the Department of Justice, legislative sponsors of CRIPA were likely to expect that vagueness would not be used by the implementing agency to limit enforcement efforts, especially since the agency had worked so hard for its passage.

CRIPA's enactment marked an intersection of efforts to ensure the authority of the federal government to vigorously enforce civil rights with the emerging concern that the government had unduly infringed upon states in its prior enforcement efforts. The procedural safeguards inserted in CRIPA to gain its passage provided statutory support for interpreting its language as promoting negotiation and conciliation over litigation, a position that meshed well with the governing philosophy of the incoming Reagan Administration.

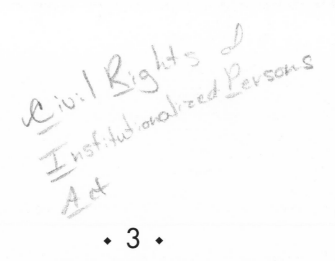

Civil Rights of
Institutionalized Persons
Act

• 3 •

Reagan Administration Ideology and the CRIPA Policy Preference

Among the most frequently-cited attributes of the Reagan management style were the clarity of the Administration's position and the relative infrequency of change or deviation in stated policies. Ronald Reagan's background and how his ideology led to the development of an administrative strategy forms the basis for examining the administrative implementation of CRIPA.

IDEOLOGY

What came to be known as *Reaganism* is traced to *The Speech*, an oft-used Reagan talk dating back to 1964, originally delivered in support of Barry Goldwater's presidential candidacy (Greenstein, 1983; Erickson, 1985, pp. 124–138). A primary theme of *The Speech* was the need to transfer power and authority from federal to state and local jurisdictions. This theme formed a fundamental and recurring part of Reagan's ideology, and it became a central focus of all of his subsequent campaigns for elective office, including his successful 1980 presidential campaign. Belief in this theme was shared by the close advisors Reagan brought to Washington, such as Edwin Meese and William French Smith (Smith, 1991). "We all basically knew what the conservative philosophy encompassed because we shared it, and had felt it evolve in ourselves and our political beliefs. After all, we were still reacting to almost two decades of FDR and his policies" (Smith, 1991, pp. 236–237).

Smith summarized the four tenets of the philosophy of Reagan and his closest aides:

1. Whether one is speaking of the political or the economic sector, ultimate responsibility should lie with the smallest entity capable of making final decisions.

2. When it comes to getting things done, emphasis should be on the private sector, not the government.

3. The best way to secure peace is to maintain a strong national defense.

4. Our democratic system requires that laws be made by our representatives, who are elected by the people themselves, and not by judges, who are appointed. (Smith, 1991, pp. xvi–xvii)

Reagan drew upon these principles in summarizing the goals for his administration in his first inaugural address, stating, "Government is not the solution to our problem; government is the problem"; "It is my intention to curb the size and influence of the Federal establishment"; and "Our present troubles parallel and are proportionate to the intervention and intrusion in our lives that result from the unnecessary and excessive growth of government" (reprinted in Nathan, 1983a, pp. 159–160). Likewise, in his first State of the Union address, President Reagan repeated his philosophy of limited government intrusion: "Together, after 50 years of taking power away from the hands of the people in their States and local communities, we have started returning power and resources to them" (reprinted in Nathan, 1983a, p. 165).

Durant (1992) identified the following ways in which the Reagan Administration implemented its philosophy:

1. Changing budget and personnel patterns in ways supportive of the President's agenda;

2. Amending, rescinding, or relaxing the enforcement of administrative regulations to suit Reagan's deregulatory instincts;

3. Appointing "movement" conservatives, intimate associates, and kindred philosophical spirits to key posts throughout the bureaucracy to direct and control its operations;

4. Pursuing major interdepartmental reorganizations designed to symbolize and institutionalize the purposes of the president;

5. Monitoring agency performance through elaborate managerial control systems; and

6. Devolving policy, enforcement, and financial responsibility for various federal programs to the states. (p. 4)

In the civil rights area, the call for states to have responsibility for monitoring and enforcing laws was not entirely new. Historically, opponents of civil rights laws often couched their opposition in the name of states' rights, perhaps driven by the belief that policy made locally would be more palatable (Bullock et al., 1983). The Reagan Administration's attitude toward civil rights enforcement was guided by the principle that the federal government should intervene as little as possible, and that past enforcement efforts exceeded the bounds of appropriate federal involvement.

Conservative supporters of the new administration made this point clearly. With respect to the Civil Rights Division of the Department of Justice, the briefing book the Heritage Foundation prepared for the new administration said: "Together with the Land Division, Civil Rights is one of the most radicalized elements of the Justice Department. In the past, attorneys in this division have used the threat of widescale resignations to intimidate conservative administrations into moderating their anti-affirmative action policies. This cannot be allowed to happen again" (Heatherly, 1981, p. 447). In the foreword to the book the Heritage Foundation prepared for his second term, President Reagan praised the assistance he received from the earlier version, stating that it gave him and his administration "special substantive help we'll never forget. . . . We've been using *Mandate* to our and our country's advantage" (Heritage Foundation, 1984, p.iii). The second briefing book contained an even more direct statement of conservative ideology: Much of what the federal government does is destructive; and many career civil servants are not to be trusted (Sanera, 1984).

The Administration's view of how "Reagan justice" should be achieved was summarized as "combating legal, political, and cultural excess, and strengthening the rule of law by recovering its original understanding and seeking new law as social conditions require" (Eastland, 1988, p. 16). How this philosophy was applied is set out in the Administration's 1983 Budget, the first it proposed. With respect to civil rights, the Budget stated:

1. Many civil rights statutes duplicated each other, creating contradictory requirements and duplicative efforts;

2. Cost effectiveness of civil rights programs was not determined;

3. Regulations were inflexible and unduly prescriptive and precluded alternative approaches;

4. Reporting requirements were excessive, and there was a failure to differentiate between compliance by large and small organizations;

5. Programs did not change with the times, failing to modify approaches that had proven unsuccessful;

6. Programs were locked into the confrontational style of the 1960's and did not build on willingness for voluntary compliance;

7. Government failed to address the problem of its own role in creating or perpetuating inequities. (Office of Management and Budget, Special Analyses, 1983, pp. J4–5)

Previous research has examined how the Reagan Administration used several of the methods identified by Durant to address these specific concerns. For example, the budget of the Civil Rights Division was altered during the Reagan Administration, although whether it increased (Reynolds, 1984a; Smith, 1991) or decreased (Shull, 1989) appears to vary by how the figures are interpreted. The Administration experienced a departure of career personnel (Schmidt & Abramson, 1983), and those positions as well as other vacancies were filled in many instances with the "kindred" spirits of Durant's list (Amaker, 1988; Brownstein & Easton, 1983; Devine, 1987; Lynn, 1984; Moe, 1985; Nathan, 1983a, 1983b; Newland, 1983; Rector & Sanera, 1987; and Smith, 1991). The general criteria for selecting Administration personnel were defined by an Administration insider as commitment to Reagan's objectives, integrity, competence, teamwork, toughness, and, later, commitment to change (Eastland, 1992). A participant in the selection process defined the criteria more concisely: "One, was he a Reagan man? Two, a Republican? and Three, a conservative?" (Brownstein & Easton, 1983, p. xvi, quoting Henry Salvatori, a member of Reagan's "kitchen" cabinet).

Much has been written about the Administration's desire to rewrite regulations, or to interpret existing law and regulations less stringently (Amaker, 1988; Bullock, 1984b; Eads & Fix, 1982; Hunter, 1987; Menzel, 1983; Nathan, 1986; Palumbo & Calista, 1990; Rector & Sanera, 1987; and Spangler, 1982). Niskanen (1987) provided the following summary of guidelines given to new appointees: "If you're ever in doubt about the policy of the Reagan Administration in a given area, the best test is probably to ask yourself: If the program or the regulation did not exist, would you expect President Reagan to create it? If the answer is no, then your long-term objective must be to eliminate the program or regulation" (p. 57). Niskanen went on to say that if the appointee were given the task of drafting regulations, they should be written as though the next Kennedy Administration were going to administer them (p. 59).

During the Reagan Administration, there was an increase in supervision and control of agency activity, lending support to Durant's observation of the creation of elaborate managerial control systems (Leadership Conference on Civil Rights, 1983; Moe, 1985; Nathan, 1983a; West & Cooper, 1985). Likewise, there is much support for the finding that there was an effort to devolve responsibility for programs to the states (Bullock, 1984b; Eads & Fix, 1982; Nathan, 1983b; Smith, 1991). An additional technique, allegedly widely used by the

Reagan Administration, is that described as "tokenism" (Bardach, 1977, p. 98), or paying lip-service to laws while not enforcing them very aggressively (Menzel, 1983; Shull & Ringelstein, 1989). This charge was vehemently denied by Reagan Administration officials (Eastland, 1988; Reynolds, 1984b, 1986). The extent to which such methods were used to achieve the Administration's policy preference toward CRIPA is examined in Chapter 4.

THE REAGAN ADMINISTRATION AND CAREERISTS

Any administration intent on effecting significant policy change is likely to view careerists in the targeted bureaucracy as obstacles to be overcome. This is true whether a Democratic administration perceives immobile bureaucratic passivity, or a Republican administration sees questionable bureaucratic neutrality (Rourke, 1992). The Reagan Administration was no exception, and conservative think tanks such as the Heritage Foundation reinforced this negative view, categorizing civil servants as opponents, reluctants, critics or even autistics (Heritage Foundation, 1984). The Reagan Administration "brought together both Carter's perspective as an outsider distrustful of Washington institutions and Nixon's suspicions that the bureaucracy was prepared to sabotage presidential initiatives with which it disagreed" (Aberbach & Rockman, 1990, p. 36).

In deciding how best to fulfill the president's agenda, a key factor for the Reagan Administration was minimizing the influence of careerists while appointing as many like-minded conservatives as possible. Prior government experience was viewed as unnecessary, and even undesirable in some instances (Ban & Ingraham, 1990). A significant aid to this strategy was the recently-enacted Civil Service Reform Act of 1978, which established the Senior Executive Service and enlarged the number of political appointments that a new administration could make. This change was designed to increase political responsiveness and give the executive new leverage over the bureaucracy (Huddleston, 1987).

Rockman (1993) contends that the goal of the Reagan strategy toward careerists was to restrict their activities to those of a non-policy nature, using micromanagement to limit their discretion. In effect, the Administration was attempting to establish a political/administrative dichotomy, or at least two strata of administrative decisionmaking—one influential and one mechanical. The effect of this strategy has been reviewed by a number of scholars. Lynn (1984) analyzes the accomplishments of five Reagan subcabinet appointees, concluding that the managerial skill and expertise of appointees charged with implementing a presidential strategy is a critical factor in their success. Heclo (1984) criticizes Lynn's work for focusing primarily on whether appointees fulfilled the president's agenda, and not on the costs of that achievement, such as the effect the strategy has on careerists.

Palumbo and Calista (1990) address the impact an aggressive administrative strategy can have on careerists in their discussion of the hostility shown by EPA employees toward Reagan and his appointees, and the effect this had on serious enforcement of environmental legislation. The careerists who remained from previous administrations were pulled in two directions. First, they were employees of the executive branch headed by a president and appointees who opposed energetic enforcement of environmental laws. Second, however, they felt they had a responsibility to carry out what they viewed to be the congressional intent that environmental legislation be vigorously enforced. "The EPA served two political masters. It could not be a single, monolithic public servant in which all members agreed on or fulfilled the same goals or objectives" (Palumbo & Calista, 1990, p. 8).

In addition to opposing administrative policy because it is perceived to differ from legislative intent, some careerists saw their role as a check upon administrative efforts to effect policy change. For example, a career attorney in the Reagan Justice Department wrote that careerists have a "duty to exert a moderating influence on appointees" (Selig, 1986, p. 788). But, the effect of policy redirection on careerists depends on the agency and the nature of the policy involved (Maranto, 1993). Certain agencies and certain policies are more likely to be staffed with persons holding strong opinions about the role of government and their agency's mission. Such persons seem especially attracted to matters of civil rights and environmental policy. In many cases, there is no consensus as to the proper scope of the agency's work, and past activity of the agency has been controversial.

Highly visible clashes, such as those engendered by Secretary of the Interior James Watt, led some analysts to conclude that the relationship between the stability fomented by careerists and the change prompted by appointees became seriously unbalanced under Reagan (Ban & Ingraham, 1990). Studies of other agencies, however, found that they responded to change in a relatively quiet and easy fashion (Golden, 1992; Kristol, 1985; Lynn, 1984). The question remains of how to administratively bring about a change in the agency's activity without causing the sort of turmoil and bureaucratic upheaval that can thwart fulfillment of the executive policy preference.

DEVELOPMENT OF A CRIPA POLICY PREFERENCE

The Department of Justice is made up of seven litigating divisions, each headed by an Assistant Attorney General. During the Reagan Administration, there were seven sections within the Civil Rights Division, each with a section chief and one or more assistants. The Special Litigation Section was charged with implementing CRIPA and enforcing Section 504 of the Rehabilitation Act of 1973. The Section had been established in 1978 to, among other things, protect the "rights to constitutionally adequate treatment and habilitation in the setting least restrictive of personal liberty for those persons" confined to various institutions (U.S. Department of Justice, 1978 Annual Report, p. 140).

William Bradford Reynolds served as Assistant Attorney General for the Civil Rights Division during the Reagan Administration, taking office on July 27, 1981, the last of the initial Department of Justice presidential appointees. The delay in the appointment was allegedly due to the Reagan Administration's unsuccessful efforts to locate a black nominee like Reynolds's predecessor, Drew S. Days, III (Brownstein & Easton, 1982). In contrast to Days, Reynolds had little prior experience in civil rights matters, coming from partnership in a Washington, D.C., law firm that specialized in commercial and regulatory litigation. The person who nominated him for a position in the Administration, Erwin Griswold, stated, "I don't think he has very broad experience in civil rights matters. But then stop and think about it for a moment: Do you think they are going to appoint someone with extensive civil rights experience to head that division?" (Brownstein & Easton, 1982, p. 399). Although not especially experienced in civil rights litigation, Reynolds possessed the requisite credentials for appointment—a belief in the Reagan ideology and a willingness to develop a corresponding civil rights policy.

Reynolds initially wanted to be the Assistant Attorney General of the Civil Division and even interviewed for that position, but instead was nominated to head Civil Rights. Although he jokingly says that he "didn't do too well in the interview" (Interview with William Bradford Reynolds, 1993), the nomination was a reflection of confidence in his ability, for the Civil Rights post had been designated for someone willing to tackle a problem area. According to Smith (1991), Edwin Meese originally opposed Reynolds's selection, instead preferring someone with more civil rights experience and a stronger political background. Smith, however, saw Reynolds's lack of knowledge in civil rights as an advantage, because Smith believed the area needed rethinking. During his interview, Reynolds was thoroughly examined about his commitment to protecting the rights of *all* citizens (Smith, 1991), a theme that resurfaced in Reynolds's later stated goal that the Justice Department would enforce the civil rights of all persons as Americans, not "as nameless representatives of some group" (Reynolds, 1984b, p. 35). This approach ran counter to what the Administration believed to be the historical Civil Rights Division mission—not just to enforce the law, but rather to fight "for" one side (Detlefsen, 1991, p. 173).

The initial civil rights agenda for the Reagan Administration Justice Department was set by Attorney General William French Smith and Deputy Attorney General Ed Schmults. This agenda derived from the Reagan theme of limited government intervention, or as summarized by the Heritage Foundation, "continu[ing] to resist attempts to increase the scope of federal regulation under the guise of civil rights" (Heritage Foundation, 1984, p. 163). Three specific civil rights policy positions conveyed were to Reynolds: The Administration was against quotas, against busing, and against the use of an "effects" test in discrimination cases (Interview with William Bradford Reynolds, 1993). Reynolds was told that his mission with respect to these issues was to figure out "how to get us from where we are today to where we want to go." Smith and Schmults told Reynolds that they were not going to handle the details; that these were the policy goals and he could decide how best to achieve them.

A key part of the Reagan Administration civil rights agenda was to frame debate in the terms that reflected its own preferences, focusing on reverse bias and unfairness to the detriment of majority interests in previous enforcement of civil rights laws. This shift in emphasis was galling to long-time civil rights enforcers within the Department, who disagreed with both the predicate and substance of the attacks on their work. For example, a Deputy Assistant Attorney General during the Carter Administration said that busing and quotas had rarely been promoted as remedies by the Justice Department, and that by singling out isolated instances the incoming Administration was engaging in a "deliberate campaign of distortion" using the "language that would poison the public mind and inflame sentiment" (Interview with Lynn Walker Huntley, 1995). The language used and issues targeted by the Administration created an atmosphere of concern and even hostility that permeated the entire Division, even in sections that were not the focus of initial attention. The main civil rights strategy was carefully monitored by Reynolds's superiors, and Reynolds said that he kept in close touch with Smith and Schmults to clear things that might be controversial.

As to CRIPA policy, however, Reynolds was generally left on his own, aside from the underlying philosophy that he was to apply to all enforcement decisions. He knew very little about CRIPA when he began, and as is customary, learned about the day-to-day work of the Division by reviewing briefing books the Sections had prepared. He found CRIPA "not a complicated statute to understand or concept to grasp" (Interview with William Bradford Reynolds, 1993). Very few in the Administration knew much about CRIPA because, Reynolds said, it didn't generate "a lot of political waves" and would only get attention if there was some type of "monumental mess-up." Reynolds went on to say that the lack of attention paid to CRIPA by others in the Administration did not necessarily indicate indifference, but was just a reflection of the fact that the focus will be first on those matters that are "beating you over the head in a very visible way."

Reynolds gleaned information from the prepared briefing books and also examined the legislative history of CRIPA. He immediately imposed a requirement that all legal pleadings filed by any section pass review by both him and one of his deputies. From the general guidelines given him by his Justice Department supervisors and the background materials on CRIPA, its legislative history, and prior Section enforcement, Reynolds developed a clear policy preference toward CRIPA soon after he was nominated, and he expressed this preference in an interview that took place shortly after his confirmation:

Basically the federal government doesn't get into the picture until it has exhausted every avenue to get the state to face up to its responsibilities. Once we're involved, our role is to make sure the minimum constitutional requirements are satisfied. Once that is done, the state is the authority which has the primary responsibility for implementing the relief and taking whatever additional steps it might want to take. . . . The change [from past policy] goes to the point in time at which one is able to strike a reasonable settlement. If a greater effort is made at the outset, it may well be that we can arrive at a meaningful resolution of the problem without spending a lot of time, energy and money litigating before we get to the point of having everybody, out of sheer exhaustion, decide they're going to sign a consent decree. (Gentry, 1981, p. 33)

The key changes from previous policies in institutional litigation were the emphasis on negotiation almost to the exclusion of litigation, and seeking to enforce only minimal constitutional requirements. Requiring treatment in the least restrictive environment, which had been stated to be one of the responsibilities of the Special Litigation Section when it was created, was never acknowledged by Reynolds to be an enforcement obligation, and indeed was rejected as a remedy that the Department could impose. These points reflect the notion that federal intervention should be a limited and last resort. When to litigate and what to seek became the focus of the CRIPA policy preference. Reynolds said the emphasis on negotiation could actually decrease the time it takes to remedy unconstitutional conditions, and that it was a dramatic change from how the Department had historically operated:

The Department . . . certainly in the Civil Rights Division, the attitude was, once we target something we know better than they, they're the bad guys, we're the good guys, there's no point in talking to 'em because . . . we don't have conversations with bad guys, and so we're gonna come after you and we're gonna hit you with all the force we can and we're gonna bring you to your knees and by damn you're gonna do what we want you to do. . . . The concern that I had with that approach in this area was it draws it out forever and you got people, you do have institutions that are not doing right. It doesn't make a whole lot of sense to take six years to litigate the case, and leave them in the kind of a situation that they're in, if in two years you can reach the result you want through a negotiated process. So, it was wrong-headed for the Division to systematically kind of target an institution and then say, we're not talking to you, we're just gonna litigate with you. . . . That's a stereotypical approach in the Department. . . . It's an "us-they," and it's a "we know better than you know." And it's that if we negotiate with these people, they're always lying to us, and they never have any interests that we have in sight, and even if we got a negotiated deal, if the court didn't tell 'em to do it they wouldn't follow it. And that's their attitude. . . . I don't buy that now, I didn't buy it then. (Interview with William Bradford Reynolds, 1993)

Although Reynolds argued that negotiation could actually achieve desired results faster than would litigation, he noted that CRIPA's legislative history showed disagreement within Congress over whether the federal government ought to be overseeing state institutions, illustrating that his concern was not limited to achieving quick results, but also went to the notion of whether the Justice Department should be involved at all. The Administration's policy preference toward CRIPA was thus formulated and implemented by Reynolds, based upon fundamental Reagan principles of limited government involvement reiterated by the Attorney General and the Deputy Attorney General.

CRIPA STUDIES

The most comprehensive summary of the Department of Justice's CRIPA enforcement activity was written by Robert Dinerstein, an attorney formerly in the Special Litigation Section. Dinerstein (1984, 1989) examined the enforcement efforts of the Special Litigation Section with respect to investigations opened, length and scope of investigations, litigation outcome, and the extent of congressional oversight, including testimony by career attorneys. Dinerstein chronicled CRIPA enforcement from the perspective of an insider who left because of differences with the Reagan Administration.

Dinerstein contends that the Reagan Justice Department retreated from the Department's "historic commitment to the protection of the civil rights of institutionalized persons" by reversing positions in landmark mental disability cases; failing to bring lawsuits, at least initially; unnecessarily prolonging investigations; adopting a limited view of which rights can be enforced; entering into formulaic and narrow consent decrees; alienating advocacy groups; causing an extreme turnover of experienced staff; and obscuring problems with CRIPA that could have been legislatively corrected (Dinerstein, 1989, pp. 388–389). Dinerstein's articles, particularly the latter one, are a rich source of data and bibliographic information. His primary focus is on the limited extent of enforcement and the possible effect of that on institutional conditions, and is therefore somewhat akin to implementation research dealing with success or failure. Criticism of CRIPA enforcement similar to Dinerstein's appeared in a review of civil rights enforcement during Reagan's first term, which concluded that the Justice Department's actions had in effect aided defendants accused of abusive or inhumane treatment of the institutionalized (American Civil Liberties Union, 1984).

A companion chapter to Dinerstein's 1989 article was co-authored by a former head of the Special Litigation Section and focused on the Section's activity with respect to prison conditions (Plotkin et al., 1989). As with the Dinerstein article, its analysis adopts the view that the Reagan Administration's limited implementation of CRIPA was improper, and supports this premise by examining the anticipated effect of Reagan policy on institutional conditions. Neither the Dinerstein nor the Plotkin articles addresses in detail the statutory features of CRIPA that facilitated the Administration's view of the scope of the law, or how the Administration was able to pursue a policy of limited enforcement without significant opposition from Congress, stakeholders, or the public.

Two other articles took a similar if less detailed approach. Cornwell (1988) subtitled his article "the failure of federal intervention for mentally retarded people," and concluded with a call to amend CRIPA to specify stricter guidelines for the initiation and progression of enforcement. The changes Cornwell proposed include the setting of a time limit for conciliation, requiring that litigation be commenced after a certain time, mandating that a public hearing be conducted prior to the entering of a consent decree, modifying the criteria for intervention, and setting standards for monitoring orders and decrees. The only other article to discuss CRIPA at any length, Killenbeck (1986), did so in less detail. Like the articles by Dinerstein and Cornwell, it focused on cases involving persons with mental disabilities.

CONCLUSION

For much of his public life, Ronald Reagan espoused the belief that, at least where domestic issues are concerned, the best government is less government, and this formed one of the guiding principles of his Administration. Appointees were questioned about and selected for their willingness to adhere to this principle. With respect to civil rights policy, appointee William Bradford Reynolds received some specific directives to challenge the civil rights orthodoxy, but was given free rein to determine how best to implement other policy preferences, including those pertaining to CRIPA enforcement. His approach toward CRIPA, as with other civil rights issues, focused on reducing intrusion on the states and separating the Justice Department from its traditional alignment with civil rights advocacy groups. The next chapter examines how Reynolds carried out this enforcement policy in directing the Justice Department's implementation of CRIPA.

• 4 •

"Special" Litigation: CRIPA
Enforcement During the Reagan
Administration

During the legislative debate on CRIPA, Carter Administration officials estimated that if the statute passed, the level of Justice Department litigation activity would remain approximately the same, meaning seven to ten lawsuits would be initiated each year. This was a logical prediction, for the purpose of enacting CRIPA was to clarify the Department's authority to file lawsuits, not to increase the number filed. Given that an investigation would precede each lawsuit, and that not all investigations would result in lawsuits, a reasonable estimate of enforcement activity under CRIPA would mean that during an eight-year, two-term administration perhaps around 100 investigations would be launched, leading to 56–80 lawsuits.

The early pace of CRIPA enforcement seemed to be on track to reach this figure. In slightly more than eight months between CRIPA's enactment and Reagan's inauguration, the Special Litigation Section began nine investigations, all the while continuing to actively litigate the many complex institutional cases that pre-dated CRIPA. In the first year of the Reagan Administration, however, only five investigations were opened. More significantly, the level of litigation did not approach the predicted rate until five or six years into the Reagan presidency, and that pace was attained only with the inclusion of cases filed simultaneously with consent decrees, meaning those that were settled when filed. A summary of all CRIPA enforcement during the Reagan Administration is contained in Appendix C.

INVESTIGATIONS AND OUTCOMES

A total of 82 investigations were initiated during the Reagan Administration, with this number fairly evenly divided among penal institutions, mental retardation facilities, and mental health institutions. In the first year, five investigations were opened; in the last full year only one was opened. In contrast, in the first year of the Ford Administration, the Department was *amicus* or intervenor in approximately 20 new cases; and in the first year of the Carter Administration, the Department initiated 11 new cases and intervened in three others (Washington Council of Lawyers, 1983).

Of the 82 CRIPA investigations opened during the Reagan Administration, 16 led to non-contested lawsuits in which a pre-negotiated proposed consent decree was filed with the Complaint. Lawsuits seeking access to institutions in order to conduct investigations occurred in three instances. In only eight instances did investigations lead to contested lawsuits, with the first being filed on February 2, 1984, more than three years after the Administration took office. The remaining investigations were either closed or still pending at the end of the Reagan Administration. The rate of CRIPA litigation during the Reagan Administration was thus one-third to one-half that predicted during legislative debate, even though the number of investigations opened was only slightly less than expected.

These numbers alone, while certainly a reflection of overall enforcement activity, tell only a portion about CRIPA enforcement. Investigations into institutional conditions involve complex issues of medicine, sanitation, safety, treatment, and even procedure, leading to divergent opinions about which conditions are unconstitutional and the scope of remedies that can be imposed. To fully understand the scope of specific CRIPA enforcement by the Reagan Administration, individual components of that enforcement must be examined.

ENFORCEMENT ISSUES

Limiting Discretion and Changing Direction

The new administration acted quickly to take steps to control and monitor the actions of its civil rights attorneys. Even prior to Reynolds's confirmation, Attorney General William French Smith ordered the Civil Rights Division to consult with and obtain the recommendation of the federal Bureau of Prisons in connection with all important pleadings involving penal conditions, whether filed in new or pending cases. The Bureau of Prisons, itself charged with operating a prison system, was seen by most civil rights attorneys as biased toward the efforts of state correctional agencies. Requiring the involvement of the historically more conservative Bureau generally was viewed by the attorneys as an additional way for the Administration to minimize the scope of federal intervention into state matters (Gentry, 1981).

Deputy Attorney General Edward Schmults was actively involved in institutional litigation in the period immediately following Reagan's inauguration. While administrative sensitivity to the views of state officials in institutional litigation is not unique to the Reagan Administration, close communication between a targeted state and Schmults, often without the knowledge of attorneys handling the cases, illustrated to many career attorneys and stakeholders undue politicization and a resulting curtailment of career attorneys' discretion. On occasion, this meant asking career attorneys to take the opposite side of an issue they had argued previously. In *Ruiz v. Estelle*, the landmark Texas prison litigation, a series of letters between Texas Governor William P. Clements, Jr., and Schmults led to a decision by the Justice Department to urge the circuit court of appeals to reverse an order the Carter Administration had supported in the district court (Leadership Conference on Civil Rights, 1983; Plotkin et al., 1989). A review of the matter by a stakeholder group reported that the line attorney in *Ruiz* was later "reprimanded summarily for not advocating the weakened position with sufficient vehemence" (Leadership Conference on Civil Rights, 1983, p. 57).

In a case involving a prison, line attorneys already in Mississippi to argue a motion regarding the housing of state prisoners in county jails learned only the day before the argument that the State had persuaded the Civil Rights Division Administration to agree to a contrary position (*Authorization Request for the Civil Rights Division of the Department of Justice*, 1982; Leadership Conference on Civil Rights, 1983). The line attorneys had not been told that the Administration was holding discussions with the State on the issue. Ultimately the court, upon its own motion, dismissed the United States from the litigation of that issue, finding that "the interests of the United States in this cause are no longer coextensive with or common to the interests of the plaintiff class" (Plotkin et al., 1989, p. 420).

Then-Mississippi State Representative, now Senate Majority Leader Trent Lott, who had been in contact with Schmults, continued to criticize the Justice Department's activity in the prison case. In a letter to Schmults, which the Department denied receiving but that nevertheless became public, Lott complained that a Department lawyer was

seeking perversely to compel even more restrictive standards on the local facilities. . . . This is contrary to common sense and to my understanding with you. I expect the situation to be corrected without delay. . . . I want to know, with reference to chapter and verse of the civil service statutes, why [the lawyer] has not been fired. There are too many lawyers ready and willing to carry out Ronald Reagan's policies to permit those policies to be subverted by mere civil servants. (Leadership Conference on Civil Rights, 1983, pp. 73–74)

In several other cases, the Department took positions that career attorneys viewed as contrary to earlier stances. In *Wyatt v. Stickney*, the Department began settlement discussions with State defendants, but excluded the plaintiffs, with whom Justice had historically been aligned. Although the court did not agree to enter the settlement negotiated by Justice, it permitted Justice to withdraw from the litigation (Dinerstein, 1989). Changes in cases like *Wyatt* were especially galling to line attorneys and stakeholders because of their symbolic significance to those in the field (Dinerstein, 1989). One rarely reads an account of such cases without seeing the word "landmark" used in association with them, and the Justice Department's involvement in *Wyatt* and other cases had been cited with approval in the Senate Report on CRIPA (S. Rep. No. 416, 1979).

Initial policy changes seemed especially visible where prisoners were concerned. In addition to retreating from positions it had taken previously in litigation, the Department deferred the implementation of rules about the redress of inmate grievances that had been promulgated pursuant to CRIPA by the Carter Administration shortly before it left office (United States Department of Justice, Office of the Attorney General, January 16, 1981). The rules were replaced with ones that imposed limits on inmate participation in certain grievances and removed requirements of full explanation of procedures and assistance to inmates (United States Department of Justice, Office of the Attorney General, July 16, 1981). This was done without providing an opportunity for public comment (Washington Council of Lawyers, 1983). Antagonism toward issues involving prisoners was openly admitted by a Deputy Assistant Attorney General: "I'm not as sympathetic surely and not very sympathetic to a lot of the things that at least at that time were being advanced and surfaced in favor of relaxing this or that requirement within the prison context" (Interview with Charles J. Cooper, 1993). Broad decrees mandating improvements in prison conditions were singled out by Attorney General Smith as an example of inappropriate judicial activism (Smith, 1991).

Change also took place in the administrative structure of the Division, where although one Section was eliminated, a Deputy Assistant Attorney General was added. The reason was clear—to provide "more efficient review and control of the litigating and legislative activities of the Division" (United States Department of Justice, Annual Report of the Attorney General, 1982, p. 153). To further increase supervision, less than one month after his confirmation Reynolds issued a directive to all civil rights attorneys, stating, "While I am in the process of reformulating current division policy in certain areas, and until further notice, I am directing that all substantive pleadings and memoranda be provided to Deputies for review at least 24 hours prior to the filing date" (Plotkin et al., 1989, p. 426). This policy was a major change in the operation of the Division. In the past, except for the initial Complaint in a lawsuit, the Sections had "pretty much [been] given carte blanche to run the case within certain parameters" (*Civil Rights of Institutionalized Persons Act Hearings*, 1983, p. 77, testimony of Robert Plotkin). Senior Trial Attorneys in the Section, those at level GS-15, by definition were given the authority to independently plan litigation strategy and to work under only the very general supervision of the Section Chief (Whinston, 1983).

Although initially the attorneys were told that the rationale for Reynolds's request was to permit him to familiarize himself with the Division's operations, the policy continued throughout both terms and was viewed by the attorneys as a way of keeping them in line (*Civil Rights of Institutionalized Persons Act Hearings*, 1983, p. 77, testimony of Robert Plotkin). Reynolds confirmed that obtaining control was the reason for the policy: "Reviewing the pleadings was very definitely an exercise that I introduced and insisted upon because there was a need to make sure that what we were saying in a court squared up with what the policy direction was" (Interview with William Bradford Reynolds, 1993).

Reynolds personally reviewed pleadings, and would return them with handwritten, detailed comments. He did not merely ask the attorneys to revise the pleadings, but would actually do major rewriting himself. This obviously altered the content of the pleadings, but also frequently resulted in tremendous delays in getting pleadings filed. A Deputy Section Chief described Reynolds's review process:

He basically took over editing every piece of paper that went out of the Civil Rights Division, causing a big bottleneck in time procedurally, which I think was intended. And secondly, he put his imprint on every document, brief, pleading, and it was a major imprint, it was total reediting, evisceration of documents, so that they were unrecognizable . . . and in some instances played very loose, we thought, with a lot of the facts and basically distorted facts in order to reach a preconceived conclusion that was compatible with his ideology. (Interview with John MacCoon, 1994)

Line attorneys were concerned with both the existence of additional review as well as with the content of that review. Generally, Reynolds's staff would review pleadings before passing them on to him, and the staff often lacked familiarity with both substantive issues and litigation practices. The first Reynolds-appointed Deputy Assistant Attorney General responsible for Special Litigation, J. Harvie Wilkinson, III, was a well-connected University of Virginia faculty member who had never tried a case in court. In one instance, Wilkinson, in reviewing the Section's proposed response to interrogatories, called in the line attorney to question him about why the Department was harassing the defendants by preparing such pleadings. He was apparently not familiar enough with the civil discovery process to recognize that the Department was the recipient, not the sender, of the pleadings he found onerous (Antonelli, 1984). In a case involving prison conditions, Wilkinson arbitrarily selected numbers for the maximum prison population and cell square-footage to be sought by Justice, with no apparent factual or legal foundation for the figures. The experienced line attorneys were baffled as to how they could justify the computation of the figures if they were called upon to do so in court (Antonelli, 1984). As one career attorney stated, "Historically, the Department's strength in institutional litigation had been the expertise and continuity it had brought to the area. Position changes undercut that continuity, and to the extent that the new positions were poorly justified, undermined any perceptions of expertise" (Dinerstein, 1989, p. 396).

Reynolds imposed a moratorium on attorneys discussing litigation with persons outside of the Department, requiring instead that inquiries be directed to a Departmental spokesman (Brownstein & Easton, 1982). The Special Litigation Section became physically more isolated when its offices were moved from the Main Justice Building on Pennsylvania Avenue to a satellite building several blocks away, the building that also housed the Bureau of Prisons. Although both the moratorium and the move can be defended as sound management decisions, these steps had the effect of limiting the contact line attorneys had with outside parties as well as the "front office," the term attorneys generally used to refer to the offices of Reynolds, his deputies, and assistants. The opinion of several attorneys is reflected by the comment of one who said that the physical isolation of the Section from the Main Justice Building "reflected the priorities of DOJ."

Review of New Section Initiatives

The Administration pursued its CRIPA policy preference through its review of Section recommendations to undertake new actions, whether opening new investigations or intervening in lawsuits brought by private parties. Due to the privileged nature of information pertaining to internal recommendations, it is impossible to compile a complete list of all such recommendations that were declined, but several have come to light through congressional testimony.

The bulk of the Department of Justice's activity in institutional cases historically had been in matters brought by private plaintiffs, where the Department's role would be that of intervenor or *amicus curiae*. The Senate Report on CRIPA recognized the value of Justice involvement in institutional cases, especially given the "limitations of resources, manpower, and continuity among publicly funded legal services and privately funded advocacy groups" (S. Rep. No. 416, 1979, p. 19). Additionally, Justice participation was recognized by the Senate as "providing expertise, credibility, conservation of judicial resources through streamlining litigation, and stability" (pp. 20–21).

With the passage of CRIPA and the Department's newly-acquired statutory authority to file its own suits, it was perhaps foreseeable that any administration would focus on new rather than ongoing litigation (Dinerstein, 1989). On the other hand, in light of the list of attributes of Justice participation contained in the Senate Report and CRIPA's explicit grant of authority to intervene and shorter periods of notice prior to intervention than prior to litigation (42 U.S.C. Section 1997c), Congress seemingly intended that the Department should continue to intervene in institutional litigation. Nevertheless, over the eight-year Reagan Administration, the Department intervened under CRIPA in only two cases, one in January, 1981 (*Santana v. Collazo*) (prior to Reynolds's arrival), and one in May, 1982 (*Davis v. Henderson*).

The reasons Reynolds gave for rejecting Section recommendations to intervene varied. In a case involving the St. Louis State School, the Missouri Association for Retarded Citizens asked Justice to intervene. The Special Litigation Section's request to do so was denied because "the private plaintiffs challenging conditions at that institution were represented by able and talented legal counsel" (Reynolds, 1983, April 20). In another case, involving a North Dakota mental retardation facility, the recommendation to intervene remained in Reynolds's office awaiting review for months. The recommendation was ultimately denied for the reason that the trial date had already been set and it was claimed by Reynolds that Justice could be little more than a bystander (Cook, 1983, October 18). Yet when the trial date was postponed, a second request to intervene was denied for the reason that "adequate time was not available to do the kind of pretrial investigation and discovery that would be required in order to participate in a meaningful way as intervenor" (Reynolds, 1983, November 16, p. 6, n.11).

A recommendation to intervene in a case involving conditions at three Idaho institutions also was denied, because Reynolds said that two of the institutions did not appear to have constitutional deficiencies, and the one that did was already the subject of litigation (Reynolds, 1983, November 16). This justification was given in spite of the fact that by definition intervention presumes ongoing litigation, and despite a note from a Deputy Assistant Attorney General suggesting that the counsel in the private case were in over their heads (*Civil Rights of Institutionalized Persons Act Hearings*, 1984). An intervention request at a Virginia mental hospital was denied because "the state was conducting its own investigation" (Washington Council of Lawyers, 1983, p. 151). Another request, one that line attorneys felt sure would be approved, was rejected because Reynolds said, "If this place is this bad, they [the private plaintiffs] don't need our help" (Interview with Section attorney).

The Reagan Administration did not intervene in any CRIPA case after May, 1982. Likewise, although Reynolds testified in 1987 that Justice was participating as *amicus* in seven institutional cases (*Authorization Request for the Civil Rights Division*, 1987), all of those cases were ones in which the decision to participate predated the Reagan Administration. Reynolds denied that he had established a new policy imposing a higher standard for intervention, stating that his policy "is remarkably similar" to that of his predecessors (Reynolds, 1983, November 16). He stated that intervention must take a lesser priority when determining how Justice should best expend its scarce resources, yet a review of Departmental budget submissions reveals no requests for additional funds in order to pursue otherwise worthy intervention requests.

CRIPA investigations are initiated by the sending of a notice letter to the state which operates the institution, informing the state that an investigation is being opened to examine allegations of unconstitutional conditions of confinement. Before that letter is sent, the Section prepares a memo to the Assistant Attorney General detailing the information it has about institutional conditions, and why that information supports the commencement of an investigation. Section attorneys are prohibited from touring the institution or contacting the state prior to the notice letter being sent, and so must rely upon reports from third parties and inspection tours that other agencies might have conducted in drafting the memo requesting that an investigation be opened. The situation is somewhat analogous to the need for probable cause before a search warrant can be issued.

Two Section recommendations to open investigations are particularly noteworthy, one involving a delay and one a denial. During the Department's participation in the *Gates v. Collier* Mississippi prison litigation, Section attorneys received information concerning conditions at the Biloxi jail. The Department filed a motion in its pending prison case asking that it be allowed to inspect the county jail in Biloxi as part of its case, because state prisoners allegedly were being housed there. Within a month of filing the motion, however, Deputy Attorney General Schmults wrote then-Mississippi State Representative Trent Lott, a Republican, telling him that the Department would hold off on its inspection if the State would provide information voluntarily. "Justice lawyers," he wrote, "would be ordered to approach the county jails issue with 'maximum possible deference to the right of Mississippi to run its own affairs without federal interference and the need to burden Mississippi with excessive compliance costs' " (Wines, 1982, November 20, p. 1998). The Section Chief later testified that the Section's request to inspect the jail had been ridiculed by Reynolds, who had stated that the "federal government had no authority to act as a roving commission" (*Civil Rights of Institutionalized Persons Act Hearings*, 1984, p. 16 [testimony of Robert Plotkin]).

After the delay caused by not being able to include the Biloxi jail in the ongoing case, the CRIPA investigation of the jail was finally approved in September, 1982. Section attorneys completed one tour of the jail with an expert, who noted fire hazards as well as other deficiencies. Two to three weeks after the tour and after the attorneys' return to Washington, the jail burned, killing 29 inmates. The Department issued a press release stating that the jail had been under investigation, but omitting any reference to the withdrawal of the motion in the *Gates* case, which would have permitted earlier inspection. In recalling the incident, a supervisory attorney who had worked on the case said in reference to Reynolds, "I remember thinking . . . 'See what your indifference can do'" (Interview with John MacCoon, 1994). Another attorney recalled the macabre experience of touring the jail once the investigation was finally approved, and seeing marks on the floor where the bodies of burned inmates had lain. Reynolds denied that political pressure had been applied to halt or delay the Biloxi jail investigation (*Civil Rights of Institutionalized Persons Act Hearings*, 1983).

The other investigation request discussed at length in congressional oversight hearings involved Hissom State School, a mental retardation facility in Oklahoma. After the request was initially denied, the Section Chief sent Reynolds a supplemental memorandum, urging him to reconsider. Reynolds again denied the recommendation, writing in his copious remarks:

The recommendation memorandum provides scanty evidence of conditions that suggest (let alone establish) "egregious and flagrant" constitutional violations. The inescapable conclusion is that Hissom is not a model institution. But little suggests that it is constitutionally deficient and no information justifies a conclusion that there are "egregious and flagrant" violations of the Constitution.

In the supplemental memorandum, reference is made to *a single death by drowning*. The incident does not suggest foul play, abusive conduct or indifference to human safety. Rather, it appears, at worst, to be a case of negligence on the part of a staff person who left a patient unattended in the tub. While the supplemental memorandum discusses this incident as "avoidable," no further discussion is provided to explain this assumption. Nonetheless, the constitutional overtones of this single incident escape me (even assuming the incident was "avoidable"). If the death fit part of a pattern of abusive and offensive treatment of residents, if it was not an isolated event that has all the earmarks of a tragic accident, rather than an inevitable consequence resulting from an "egregious" course of conduct by staff personnel, then constitutional concerns could be implicated, even without more. But the Hissom environment—even in terms of the "totality of circumstances" . . . does not begin to fit that mode. (*Civil Rights of Institutionalized Persons Act Hearings*, 1983, p. 217)

Thus, Reynolds would not authorize the opening of an investigation into whether unconstitutional conditions existed because the attorneys could not persuade him that unconstitutional conditions existed, leading many attorneys and persons familiar with the field to conclude that the Department had adopted a new, restrictive standard for initiating cases. As one Section attorney put it, "It was almost as though you needed as much information for a preinvestigation as for an investigation." Another concluded, "Not only did Reynolds and Wilkinson avoid venturing into new areas, they ran backwards, refusing to participate in cases that the Administration normally would have taken" (Antonelli, 1984, p. 47, quoting David Vanderhoof). When the Administration did approve investigations, it took a more limited view of the relief it was authorized to pursue.

Scope of Remedies

Historically, the remedies sought by the Justice Department in institutional litigation were relatively broad and varied. In prison litigation, the relief was that which had been developed through litigation interpreting the eighth amendment's proscription against cruel and unusual punishment. With respect to cases involving mental retardation or mental health facilities, the case law had not been as well circumscribed, but generally involved the application of the standard expressed by the Supreme Court in *Jackson v. Indiana* (1972), that "due process requires that the nature and duration of commitment bear some reasonable relation to the purpose for which the person is committed" (p. 738). In other words, the confinement in an institution of nondangerous mentally ill or retarded persons can be justified only if they are provided treatment or care. Litigation that developed in the wake of *Jackson* wrestled with how to define the type of treatment or care required by the Constitution.

In congressional testimony given during an oversight hearing on an unrelated statute, a former Chief of the Special Litigation Section gave examples of the types of remedies that would be sought under CRIPA, if enacted. The remedies included: ensuring that persons were evaluated on an individual basis; that institutions comported with current generally accepted professional standards of care; that buildings are kept clean and conducive to good health; and that medications are not used as punishment, for convenience, as a substitute for programming, or in a quantity that interferes with residents' functioning (*Oversight Hearings on Title I*, 1980, testimony of Mary Lynn Walker).

Judicial remedies arising from the recognition of a right to treatment resulted in the imposition of detailed injunctions (*Wyatt v. Stickney*), as well as deinstitutionalization, primarily moving persons out of institutions into community placements (*New York State Association for Retarded Children v. Rockefeller*).

It was in an environment of a generally recognized right to treatment that the Supreme Court agreed to consider a case involving an institutionalized mentally retarded man, Nicholas Romeo. In *Youngberg v. Romeo* (1982), issued on June 18, the Court held that under the fourteenth amendment an institutionalized person has, in addition to adequate food, shelter, clothing, and medical care, the rights to safe conditions, freedom from unreasonable bodily restraint, and to receive the training necessary to ensure the first two rights. A concurrence by Justice Blackmun would add to those three a constitutional right to the training needed to prevent basic self-care skills from deteriorating, but this was not a remedy sought by plaintiff Romeo. Blackmun also said he would recognize a right to treatment if treatment were the basis for the commitment.

Chief Justice Burger, in a separate concurrence, stated that in his view the majority's opinion reflected the outer limits of an institutionalized person's constitutional rights, and that there was no right to treatment per se. The majority opinion thus listed the rights plaintiff Romeo had, without saying whether he could also have others in addition to the ones he sought; Blackmun's concurrence said there were definitely other rights beyond those specifically sought; and Burger's concurrence said there were no rights beyond those listed.

Six days after the *Youngberg* opinion was issued, Reynolds sent the Special Litigation Section a memorandum interpreting the decision and setting forth guidelines for future CRIPA enforcement. The memorandum took Section Chief Arthur Peabody by surprise, especially because through a clerical error it was sent over first as a draft handwritten by Reynolds (Interview with Arthur Peabody, 1994). The memo essentially adopted the Burger concurrence, holding that *Youngberg* established the maximum constitutional limits for redressing conditions at institutions, and directing that future investigations should not examine whether institutions were providing "psychiatric care, psychological treatment or individualized therapeutic efforts designed to enhance capacity, capability and competence" (Reynolds, 1982, June 24, p. 2).

This memo was a significant turning point in CRIPA enforcement. It was one of the few written statements of Administration policy, and it was issued so quickly after the Court's decision that few attorneys had had an opportunity to read and interpret *Youngberg* for themselves. While the general topic of which rights were constitutionally based had been part of an ongoing discussion between the Section and the front office, the June 24 memo itself had been drafted and issued without seeking review and comment from the Section (Interview with Arthur Peabody, 1994). The memo adopted the narrowest possible reading of the Supreme Court decision, reinforcing the opinion of many that the Administration had abandoned its role as a civil rights advocate. In addition to interpreting *Youngberg* narrowly, for the seasoned trial attorneys the memo reflected Reynolds's unfamiliarity with some of the nuances in the field: "If you review the memo it does, irrespective of his determination as to what the policy ought to be, indicate a fair lack of awareness of a lot of the concepts that are relevant. I mean there's one section of the memo . . . that indicates there should be no psychological services, and no this and no that, and no whatever, which even his own narrow reading of *Youngberg* would require" (Interview with Arthur Peabody, 1994).

Section attorneys responded in a memo over Section Chief Peabody's name. Calling Reynolds's interpretation "unnecessarily restrictive," the memo asserted that the Section could still seek rights equal to those recognized in *Youngberg*, rights broader than those listed in the Reynolds memo, as well as rights "recognized by other courts and not precluded by the decision" (Peabody, 1982, p. 1). The difference in perspective between Reynolds and the Section was a variation on the "is-the-glass-half-full-or-half-empty" analogy: "Rather than view the decision as the floor beneath which states should not go, Mr. Reynolds treated *Youngberg* as the ceiling above which the courts must not go" (Dinerstein, 1989, p. 393).

The reaction of career attorneys and stakeholders to the *Youngberg* memo will be examined in greater detail in the next two chapters. Its strategic significance was to anchor the debate over the meaning of *Youngberg* in the context favored by the Administration, in a manner that precluded much meaningful input from career attorneys, and to use the resulting framework as the basis for restricting the remedies sought in institutional litigation. Reynolds would use *Youngberg* to deflect criticism, saying, for example, at a congressional hearing, that the policy decisions he made were "compelled by what the Supreme Court has told us to do" (*Civil Rights of Institutionalized Persons Act Hearings*, 1984, p. 125).

During the remainder of the Administration, Reynolds relied on his interpretation of *Youngberg* to avoid seeking such remedies as a right to treatment, the use of special masters, redressing the loss of abilities over the period of institutionalization, and community placement, all previously included in Justice Department litigation, contending that such matters had not been sanctioned by *Youngberg*. But as Dinerstein (1989) noted, "Of course, these issues did not arise in *Youngberg*" (pp. 700–701). The Supreme Court typically limits its holdings to those matters specifically asserted by the parties, and since Romeo had not sought any of those remedies, they were not addressed in the Court's opinion. Reynolds used the Court's silence on these remedies as an indication that the Court did not consider them to be constitutionally required. It is difficult to prove this view wrong; at best it can be said that it does not apply traditional case analysis. A congressional staff report critical of Reynolds's CRIPA enforcement conceded that "the arguments presented by the DOJ do not appear to directly contradict the Supreme Court's holding in *Youngberg*," but went on to say "they are a restrictive interpretation of the case and one which is contrary to arguments presented by commentators and several recent judicial interpretations" (*Care of Institutionalized Mentally Disabled Persons*, Part 2, 1985, p. 245). An attorney who left Special Litigation reflected the impression of many: "The bottom line would always be the most restrictive interpretation possible, one that would afford people that we were supposed to be representing the least rights possible" (Antonelli, 1984, p. 47, quoting Steve Whinston).

Although the *Youngberg* memo was scrutinized by Congress and stakeholder groups, another significant policy decision was implemented in relative obscurity, perhaps because of the absence of a memo elucidating it. CRIPA gives the Attorney General the right to sue states if persons confined in non-correctional facilities are subjected to conditions which deprive them of "rights, privileges, or immunities secured or protected by the Constitution *or laws* of the United States" (42 U.S.C. Section 1997a(a) [emphasis added]). Thus for mental retardation or health facilities, a CRIPA investigation could encompass violations of federal law as well as constitutional deficiencies. Despite this express authorization and the efforts of Section attorneys, litigation under CRIPA rarely included claims arising under federal law, even though many facilities could have been cited for violations of Section 504 of the Rehabilitation Act, the Education for Handicapped Children Act, and others. No rationale for this decision was given by Reynolds or other members of the Administration. A Section attorney who was frustrated in his efforts to seek such remedies pointed out that, although there could arguably be a philosophical difference over the scope of constitutional rights that could be sought, there is no such philosophical basis for omitting the redress of federal statutory rights in CRIPA investigations (Interview with Section attorney).

The change in what could be included in investigations into unconstitutional conditions was accompanied by a change in how those investigations would be conducted and what outcome would be sought.

Conducting Investigations

CRIPA contains specific time limits before certain actions can be taken. Seven days' notice must be given before starting an investigation, and at least 49 days must pass between a letter setting out deficiencies and the filing of a lawsuit. The statute thus provides a period of notice so that the state can have a reasonable opportunity to remedy unconstitutional conditions. The Senate Report accompanying CRIPA made it clear that the Attorney General need not "wait months or years between the initial notification of commencement of an investigation and the filing of suit" (S. Rep. No. 416, 1979, p. 815). Indeed, the Report noted that one purpose of CRIPA was to accelerate the pace of litigation or settlement, "thus saving weeks or months of discovery and trial" (p. 805). Yet negotiation seemed to be the preferred course of the Reagan Administration even if a state was dilatory in its response.

The time it took the Administration to take steps in negotiations became a source of some controversy. Appendix C shows the time elapsed between the initiation of the investigation, the issuance of findings, and the filing of a contested lawsuit or consent decree for each investigation that resulted in one of those actions, or was still pending at the end of the last full fiscal year of the Reagan Administration. The vast majority of investigations took between one and two years from investigation to findings, as well as from findings to resolution. Some cases are especially noteworthy for their duration.

The investigation of the Cummins Unit of the Arkansas Prison System began in September 1985, and was still pending at the end of fiscal year 1988 (September 30, 1988). The investigation of another prison facility, Folsom State Prison in California, lasted from August 1980, until April 1984, when findings were issued. The investigation was ultimately closed in March 1985, because steps taken in a private lawsuit were seen as adequate to protect inmates' rights (U. S. Department of Justice, Civil Rights Division, 1985). Lengthy investigations also occurred in facilities where constitutional deficiencies were not redressed in private litigation. In the case of Atascadero State Hospital in California, deficiency findings were issued in May 1984, 22 months after the investigation was initiated. The Fiscal Year 1988 Report on CRIPA enforcement noted only that the Section continued to monitor the State's efforts to address deficiencies.

The duration of the investigation of the Rosewood Center, a Maryland mental retardation facility, was examined and criticized in several congressional hearings. Rosewood was the facility at issue in the *United States v. Solomon* case, the dismissal of which illustrated the need for the passage of CRIPA. Rosewood, not surprisingly, was the subject of one of the first investigations opened under CRIPA, in November 1980. Deficiency findings were issued in February 1982, but it took until January 1985 to file a lawsuit along with a consent decree. The Justice Department report for as late as Fiscal Year 1987 noted the existence of "deficiencies that have not yet been corrected as prescribed" (p. 33).

The time involved in conducting investigations reflected the stated preference of the Administration for negotiation in lieu of litigation, and was also the natural result of the time involved in having close review of pleadings and recommendations, subsequent editing and follow-up, and also self-censorship by Section management and staff hesitant to pursue what might be viewed as close cases. Although the emphasis on negotiation had support in the language and the legislative history of CRIPA, the Administration emphasized negotiation almost to the exclusion of litigation. The 1982 Report of the Attorney General, in a recitation of activities of the Civil Rights Division, said, "The Division continued its policy of providing notice to states before it commenced litigation. This practice was extensively used in resolving conditions found in state facilities during investigations under the Institutionalized Persons Act" (p. 153). That report also listed the giving of prior notice to states as a priority activity of the Section. A statutory procedure was thus transformed into a departmental policy, placing the giving of notice to states on the same plane as redressing unconstitutional conditions.

This perspective also was reflected in the major objectives of the Section, as set out in the Department's annual authorization request. In its 1984 Budget document, the Department listed the following major objectives: "To investigate, upon reasonable cause, the conditions of confinement and treatment provided to persons in publicly operated institutions. *As a last resort*, to initiate civil actions on behalf of persons confined to publicly operated institutions wherein egregious conditions deprive them of their constitutional or federal statutory rights" (*Departments of Commerce, Justice, and State, the Judiciary, and Related Agencies Appropriations for 1985*, 1984, p. 1411, 1984 [emphasis added to denote changes from prior year's submission]). Included in the 1988 Budget Request was a statement of the Administration's view of CRIPA: "The entire concept of CRIPA is based on the government's desire to ensure rights within these facilities in agreement with the states involved and without resorting to litigation" (*Departments of Commerce, Justice, and State, the Judiciary, and Related Agencies Appropriations for 1988*, 1987, p. 555).

Former Section Chief Robert Plotkin, critical of the Administration's reliance on statutory language about negotiation to justify extended investigations, testified before Congress that the time limits contained in CRIPA were not so lengthy as to be significant, and were "not unlike DOJ's customary prelitigation practices . . . in most of its litigation activities (*Civil Rights of Institutionalized Persons Act Hearings*, 1983, p. 10 (testimony of Robert Plotkin)). As one of the House sponsors of CRIPA put it during the same hearing, "Part of the quid pro quo was to assure the States that there wouldn't be a flood of litigation. . . . But it was not the purpose of those rules to prevent litigation or to necessarily proceed in any other way" (p. 115, testimony of Rep. Robert Kastenmeier).

Plotkin said that one effect of the Administration's posture is that when so much time is spent conducting investigations, states will not take the Department's actions very seriously, especially when there is little chance that the investigations will result in litigation.

As any practicing lawyer will tell you, efforts to negotiate are never going to be very successful unless the people with whom you are negotiating believe that at the end of that process, if you are not going to get most or part of what it is you are looking for, if you are not going to file a lawsuit, if you are not going to be vigorous and aggressive in protecting the rights of essentially your clients, then there is no incentive on the part of the States to negotiate, discuss, and make improvements. (*Civil Rights of Institutionalized Persons Act Hearings*, 1983, p. 5 (testimony of Robert Plotkin))

The Department's rapid action in the so-called "Baby Doe" cases also handled by the Special Litigation Section, involving the right of disabled newborns to receive treatment, buttressed the belief of some careerists that the emphasis on negotiation in CRIPA cases was an indication of antipathy toward the statute, rather than a universal policy of deference to states (Dinerstein, 1984). In other words, federalism concerns predominated when the Administration did not support a statute, but fell by the wayside when the federal government was addressing an issue promoting a conservative ideology, such as the Baby Doe cases that implicated pro-life concerns. Such inconsistencies made it difficult for careerists to believe that the Administration's reliance on negotiation in CRIPA investigations was advanced in good faith.

Reynolds and his staff did not initially involve themselves in the day-to-day conduct of investigations, leaving line attorneys free to select the type, number, and identity of expert witnesses to accompany Section attorneys on tours and issue the detailed reports upon which findings were based. Over time, however, some persons who had served as experts refused requests to become involved, citing "concern that they would be unduly limited in their assessment of institutional conditions to the narrow issues the Department chose to investigate" (Dinerstein, 1989, p. 407). Additionally, at some point in the mid-1980s the front office imposed a procedure that precluded the Section from selecting its own experts, requiring them instead to submit a list of names from which the front office could select (Interview with Arthur Peabody, 1994). Although indicative of the managerial controls imposed on the Section, Peabody felt that in the long run this did not greatly affect investigations as the Section could still select the names of persons who appeared on the submitted list.

Once an investigation resulted in deficiency findings, the Section had the task of determining what action it should take next, in light of the steps likely to be acceptable to Reynolds. This weighing of concerns developed into another characteristic of CRIPA enforcement—a generic, formulaic consent decree filed with the lawsuit.

Consent Decrees

The use of consent decrees to resolve complex institutional litigation is not unique to the Reynolds era. Both Reynolds's predecessor, Drew Days, and Section Chief Arthur Peabody stated that negotiation has historically been used to resolve such matters (Gentry, 1981; Interview with Arthur Peabody, 1994). The differences under Reynolds were two-fold—the amount of time spent negotiating (discussed above), and the content of the final product.

The first CRIPA consent decree to be negotiated and filed with a court was in the case of *United States v. Indiana*, involving conditions in two Indiana mental health facilities. Reynolds was personally involved, having flown with attorneys to Indianapolis to meet with Indiana's Governor during the course of the investigation. As a result of his interest and the involvement of a particularly persuasive staff attorney with an academic background in mental health issues, the resulting consent decree, although somewhat general, contained specifics about fire safety and types of staff, requirements that were absent from later decrees.

The *Indiana* case also set the pattern for how investigations would be resolved. The CRIPA investigation would be conducted, a "49-day" letter outlining deficiencies would be sent, settlement negotiations would follow, and the process would culminate in the submission to the court of a proposed consent decree the same day the litigation was commenced, along with a motion to dismiss the case upon the entry of the consent decree. There would be no litigation per se in such cases, unless the defendants were later charged with contempt of the consent decree.

The Reynolds approach to settling cases is best illustrated by the events surrounding the filing of a consent decree concerning the Michigan prison system, the first prison decree negotiated under Reynolds. The staff attorneys involved in the investigation negotiated with state officials and developed a 54-page proposed decree, similar to those that had been entered in other prison cases in which Justice had been involved. The attorneys negotiating the decree had kept the Section Chief informed of their progress, which also had been discussed generally with Reynolds. The decree was agreed to by the Attorney General and the Governor of Michigan, as well as by all key persons at the correctional facilities involved, steps taken in part to ward off Administration criticism that the remedies unduly infringed upon the state. The attorneys then took the decree back to Washington to obtain approval from Reynolds.

Reynolds summarily rejected the decree and returned it to the Section. The Section Chief gave it to other attorneys to rewrite, and they drafted a six-page document, with an attached plan incorporating many of the matters contained in the original decree. In a handwritten notation explaining the rejection, Reynolds stated that "federal supervision of most planned improvements goes well beyond our proposed Complaint and our CRIPA authority" *(Civil Rights of Institutionalized Persons Act Hearings*, 1984, p. 433). The revised decree made it clear that the detailed plan was not a "specification *per se* of constitutionally required acts on the part of the state," and that "defendants' failure to comply with the provisions of the plan without more shall not be construed as a constitutional violation of any sort whatever" (p. 437).

The rewritten decree and the proposed Complaint, minus the name of one of the original attorneys and with another's name crossed out, were sent back to the Michigan officials, who signed off on the decree. The Complaint and proposed decree were filed on January 18, 1984. Counsel for private plaintiffs involved in a separate prison conditions suit and the ACLU National Prison Project were permitted by the court to participate and to oppose the entry of the consent decree, over Justice's objection. An expert who had been employed by Justice to investigate prison conditions filed an affidavit with the court, calling the proposed decree no more than "a set of polite suggestions" (Alexander, 1984, p. 5). On March 23, 1984, the judge rejected the proposed decree, stating:

The point is that in its present form it seems to me that I do nothing by signing the five-page consent decree. I don't know what it means, and if I don't know what it means, I can't see how anyone else does. And I agree with one of the lawyers who argued I will have to litigate this case from now until the end of my term inasmuch as I will not be able to understand what it is (a) that is claimed to be a constitutional violation, and (b) if it is a constitutional violation, what it is that I am supposed to do or what evidence I am going to have to hear to make a determination if that really happened. . . . [T]he decree as I read it is inadequate. It says very little. It is impossible for me to know what has been agreed upon, and I don't know how such an agreement is to be enforced. (*United States v. Michigan*, 1987, pp. 947–948)

The judge ordered the parties to negotiate a new decree. Michigan prepared a decree that made the entire plan enforceable; Justice proposed an eight-page decree (Alexander, 1984, p. 5). The judge ordered Michigan's attorneys to go to Washington to negotiate with Reynolds directly, but Justice again submitted the same eight-page decree. Reynolds himself then appeared in court to argue for the decree's entry. The judge finally accepted the decree after ordering changes that increased his role in reviewing proposed modifications, scheduling a hearing to oversee the implementation of the decree, and allowing the National Prison Project and private plaintiffs to assist in monitoring compliance.

Following the Michigan experience, the Department adopted what line attorneys called a "cookie-cutter" approach for future decrees. All decrees had a similar format, with little or no variation in remedies regardless of the specific conditions of the institutions that were the subject of the decrees (Interview with Section attorney). The rights of the institutionalized would be defined in the narrowest terms possible, mechanisms for enforcement would be scant, and there would be no provision for short-term relief (Dinerstein, 1989). The general goal in each decree would be "to bring each of these conditions to the minimum level required by the Constitution of the United States," but exactly what that level was would not be specified (*Care of Institutionalized Mentally Disabled Persons*, Part 2, 1985, p. 161). The result was that states agreed to be bound by the Constitution, an empty promise because they were already supposed to be in compliance with constitutional requirements. The lack of specificity as to what was constitutionally required made it difficult for the Department to ever prove in a contempt hearing that an institution was violating a decree (Dinerstein, 1989).

The Michigan experience also illustrated an inconsistency in the Administration's posture of allowing states to determine their own remedies. Although the State of Michigan had agreed to the 50-page mandatory decree, the Department insisted that it be governed instead by a six-page, discretionary plan. Such insistence ignored the possibility that states would prefer to know precisely the terms with which they must comply. A former attorney noted, "This incident proves that Reynolds does not want cooperation—where he gets cooperation, he still undermines everything that advocates for institutionalized persons attempt to accomplish" (*Enforcement of Section 504 of the Rehabilitation Act*, 1983, pp. 169–170 (testimony of Timothy Cook)). Ironically, the decree's vagueness enabled the federal judge, a former civil rights activist, to expand his oversight beyond that to which he could have been limited had the decree been more specific.

The concern over saving states from themselves also surfaced in the Department's actions in institutional litigation initiated prior to the Reagan Administration. In a case involving conditions at a Connecticut mental retardation facility, Deputy Assistant Attorney General Wilkinson had to urge Reynolds not to object to a proposed settlement negotiated between the plaintiff (an advocacy group) and the state: "For the Department to strip this proposal of everything the state itself was willing to offer the handicapped would be unseemly, to put it mildly" (*Civil Rights of Institutionalized Persons Act Hearings*, 1984, p.761 (memorandum from J. Harvie Wilkinson to William Bradford Reynolds)). When asked at a congressional hearing to respond to criticism leveled at his emphasis on negotiation, Reynolds stated that his objective was "to provide relief required under the Act to the greatest number of people in the shortest period of time." To do so, he explained, litigation should be the remedy of last resort. "If successful, the rights of institutionalized persons receive the full measure of constitutional protection far more rapidly and comprehensively than could ever be accomplished through protracted litigation" (*Care of Institutionalized Mentally Disabled Persons*, Part 1, 1985, pp. 402–403).

The Administration also took steps to limit the monitoring of state compliance efforts, opposing the appointment of special masters, who historically had been used to assist courts in overseeing complex litigation (Dinerstein, 1989; *United States v. Michigan*, 1987). Additionally, the form consent decrees provided that once a state believes it has achieved compliance, it may move to dismiss the case. Although the burden of proof would typically be on the moving party, these decrees provided that the burden would then fall on the United States to demonstrate that the state had not fully and faithfully implemented the decree or plan, *and* that the area of noncompliance was essential to achievement of one of the decree's general principles (*Civil Rights of Institutionalized Persons Act Hearings*, 1984, pp. 450–455 (Michigan consent decree)). Such language makes it difficult to successfully oppose a state's motion to dismiss: "Once we entered the consent decree, we didn't have any way, an effective way to enforce it. Because the hoop you had to jump through to try to get any kind of contempt was massive, counterproductive. And the decree was so broadly written, it was so hard to say you're in violation. It was just like starting the case over again" (Interview with Section attorney). If a special master or advisory panel is not appointed, the Department bears the primary responsibility for reviewing compliance. Whether due to a lack of resources or interest, the effort made to monitor compliance of CRIPA decrees was relatively slight (Cornwell, 1988).

There are examples of consent decrees with stronger enforcement language. The consent decree in *United States v. Massachusetts*, involving Worcester State Hospital, was arrived at after a trial on the merits, a circumstance that could provide documented justification for getting Reynolds to agree to stronger enforcement measures (Dinerstein, 1989). A consent decree addressing conditions at Fairview Training Center and taking a sympathetic view toward community placement efforts came about after a personal tour by Reynolds of the institution and community facilities. Reynolds had a greater interest in remedies at that facility, in part due to a memorable encounter he had with a three-year-old girl during a tour of the facility (Interview with William Bradford Reynolds, 1993; Interview with Section attorney).

The duration of the settled cases (only one of which had been totally dismissed by a court at the end of the Reagan Administration) is comparable to the duration of traditional litigation, but with a smaller scope. Undoubtedly, such efforts changed some institutional conditions for the better, but these changes were by definition less broad than changes imposed in cases litigated by previous administrations.

BUDGET OF THE SPECIAL LITIGATION SECTION

With the enactment of CRIPA, Congress envisioned that there would be a need for increased appropriations to hire more attorneys and experts to conduct investigations, and the final budget request of the Carter Administration reflected that need, requesting two additional attorneys for the Special Litigation Section and a further increase of $100,000 to pay experts (*Departments of Commerce, Justice, and State, the Judiciary, and Related Agencies Appropriations for 1981*, 1980). Over the entire Reagan Administration, however, there was no further significant increase or decrease in the amount requested for Special Litigation, save for the 1988 Budget which asked for an additional $120,000 for the cost of expert consultants (*Departments of Commerce, Justice, and State, the Judiciary, and Related Agencies Appropriations for 1983–1989*, 1982–1988).

Given that many of the decisions that he made were ostensibly based on the Division's need to conserve scarce resources, Reynolds was asked why the Department never submitted a budget requesting more attorneys and money for CRIPA enforcement:

It was a matter of Congress's priorities. What you have to do is calculate where they would give you more attorneys. You knew they'd give you more in the voting rights area, because . . . you could point to and say, look we've got this overload—we have to deal with it, you don't have a choice, we're the only game in town. Section 5 preclearance has to be done. . . . I think in the Criminal area we were able to get some. You come to institutionalized persons, you'd like five more. They say, we've already given you five. So it, both in terms of the internal budget that was put together in the White House, and in terms of Congress, that was a game that everybody was playing where you were doing, you were maximizing your ability to get more people wherever you put them. (Interview with William Bradford Reynolds, 1993)

Reynolds went on to say that in one instance, he was able to shift a position slated for another Section to Special Litigation.

The Section Chief has a different recollection of the actual positions and budget. While the stated budgetary amount did not decrease over time, the actual determination of how the money was allocated among the Sections was done by the leadership of the Civil Rights Division. According to Section Chief Arthur Peabody, after the early departures of attorneys, the Special Litigation

Section ended up losing approximately eight positions, because "there was a great opportunity after all those people left to reorder those in terms of the size of the offices" (Interview with Arthur Peabody, 1994). There was thus what Peabody termed a "significant decrease" in the number of positions in Special Litigation. All of this reordering was done internally, and was not apparent from the yearly appropriation requests. While Peabody did not recall the "juggling" of a position referred to by Reynolds, he said that if it indeed had occurred, it had a minimal impact in comparison to the losses that the Section sustained early in the Administration. Despite a reduction in litigation activity, Peabody stated that during the Reagan Administration there were never enough attorneys to do the work of the Section.

Although the public record shows no clear strategy with respect to the budget of the Special Litigation Section, in practice the allocations reflect the relatively low priority given to the Section, even in contrast to other Sections in the Civil Rights Division.

STAFFING DECISIONS

Reynolds could influence the selection of two types of staff—his own appointed staff of deputies and special assistants, and the career attorneys in the Special Litigation Section itself. He was given free rein from his superiors to make his staff decisions (Interview with William Bradford Reynolds, 1993). During the course of the Administration, Reynolds selected three deputy assistant attorney generals with line authority over the Special Litigation Section, as well as Special Assistants who frequently served as the first line of review outside of the Section (Interview with Arthur Peabody, 1994). All of the persons chosen by Reynolds were ideologically conservative, white males.

Reynolds's first selections in this area were J. Harvie Wilkinson, III, as Deputy, and Charles J. Cooper as Special Assistant. Wilkinson was a former law clerk to Supreme Court Justice Lewis F. Powell, Jr., a protegé of former Virginia Governor Linwood Holton, a former Republican candidate for Congress, an editor of *The Virginian-Pilot* in Norfolk, and a faculty member at the University of Virginia School of Law. Although unquestionably bright, he was brought to Justice having never tried a case or even practiced law (Antonelli, 1984). Reynolds explained the decision by saying, "He was a friend . . . I knew some things he'd done, and I knew where he was coming from" (Interview with William Bradford Reynolds, 1993). Wilkinson's unfamiliarity with legal procedure led to the previously-related anecdotes about his naiveté concerning court procedures, but those concerns were overshadowed by internal criticism that "he reasons from the bottom up. He doesn't decide what the questions should be until he already has decided the answers" (Antonelli, 1984, p. 47).

Wilkinson left the Department in August of 1983, and later that year was appointed to the U.S. Court of Appeals for the Fourth Circuit, although the confirmation process took several months due to delays occasioned by the need to accommodate opponents who wished to testify. Though criticized by some line attorneys, a Deputy Section Chief had some favorable comments about Wilkinson:

His heart was in the wrong place, it was there with Reynolds, but he was a nice guy. . . . I certainly didn't perceive him as a threat to my job, in fact he was just the opposite. . . . He was the type of person who, had Reagan wanted to appoint someone whom we, though we disagreed with, could have respected and worked with, should have been appointed, because he was courteous and just basically a decent person and kind enough to be able to disagree with people without considering them the enemy or making them feel threatened. (Interview with John MacCoon, 1994)

Shortly after Wilkinson's departure, Charles (Chuck) Cooper was moved from Special Assistant to Deputy Assistant Attorney General. An Alabamian, he was a former law clerk to Supreme Court Justice William Rehnquist and had worked on the Reagan campaign in Georgia. After the 1980 election, he had simply sent in his resumé to the incoming administration, and was hired. He had no prior experience in civil rights (Interview with Charles Cooper, 1993). He initially served as Reynolds' chief staff attorney, and concentrated on implementing the variety of policy changes in all areas of civil rights (Ball & Greene, 1985).

Cooper and Reynolds developed a personal friendship, and would spend time together in the office and on their daily runs on the Mall (Kmiec, 1992). Although it was said that Cooper could at times be "quite charming" (Interview with Arthur Peabody, 1994), his replacement of Wilkinson ushered in a more hostile atmosphere: "Chuck was a lot like Brad, basically . . . equally, let's say, personally offensive. I mean, someone who had no tact or any desire to try to get along with people. And all they cared about is getting their views in place and implemented, and basically were rude people. And Chuck would do it with this big smile on his face, you know, and Brad would kind of clench teeth or something, but both of them were just rude, insensitive people" (Interview with John MacCoon, 1994).

Cooper continued to have responsibility for Special Litigation until his appointment to and confirmation as the Assistant Attorney General in charge of the Office of Legal Counsel in late 1985. In his confirmation hearing, he stated that he and Reynolds "approached a broad range of policy issues from a similar philosophical outlook" (*Confirmation Hearings on Federal Appointments*, Part 2, 1985, p. 580).

Cooper's role with respect to Special Litigation was taken over by Mark Disler, who later worked on Senator Orrin Hatch's staff. Although Disler's involvement was less influential than either Wilkinson's or Cooper's, he was characterized as more of a problem because he had less knowledge and experience (Interview with Arthur Peabody, 1994). Hugh "Joe" Beard, who was another Special Assistant appointed by Reynolds, had been a deputy counsel in the U.S. Department of Education. As a private attorney in the 1970s, he had worked on reverse discrimination cases challenging Justice Department efforts to increase minority enrollment in higher education (Ball & Greene, 1985). In describing the frustration she felt after trying to convince Beard to approve a particular approach in a case, one attorney characterized Beard's attitude toward the mentally retarded by saying he was the sort of person who thought "in prehistoric times, these people would have been eaten by saber-toothed tigers and that was what should happen now . . . the milk of human kindness did not flow through him" (Interview with Section attorney). Due to Beard's philosophical outlook, Peabody called him "quite a challenge" (Interview with Arthur Peabody, 1994).

After his confirmation, Reynolds immediately had to fill the Section Chief position in Special Litigation after the departure of Robert Plotkin, effective July 31, 1981. Reynolds put Arthur Peabody in the job in an acting capacity. Peabody was a career Special Litigation attorney who had been Deputy Section Chief since 1978. To replace Peabody, Reynolds brought John MacCoon, a career civil rights attorney, from another section and appointed him Acting Deputy Section Chief.

Reynolds kept both men in their acting capacities for some time. Peabody's appointment was not made permanent until May 1983, a period of time he characterizes as possibly "historic." MacCoon likewise was kept acting, and MacCoon recalls his acting status as being even longer than was Peabody's. Both Peabody and MacCoon credit Wilkinson with ultimately convincing Reynolds to make their appointments permanent (Interview with John MacCoon, 1994; Interview with Arthur Peabody, 1994).

Although Reynolds could have retained supervisory personnel in acting capacities in part to keep the Section "in line," only one Section supervisor appears to have been appointed for his perceived ability to rein in opposition within the Section. Benjamin Schoen was a lateral hire from the Civil Division, and was selected to replace John MacCoon in 1984. He was the only Special Litigation hire interviewed personally by Charles Cooper (Interview with Charles Cooper, 1993). Although Reynolds never told Schoen directly that his mission was to take a particular managerial stance, Schoen said he believed that task was "implicit," and he set out to closely scrutinize and edit the work of line attorneys, limiting arguments that would be included in pleadings sent to the front office and in the process creating more delay in pursuing remedies. (Interview with Benjamin Schoen 1994). Several of the attorneys interviewed pointed to Schoen as an even more difficult barrier to overcome than Reynolds, for they viewed him as an appointed "gatekeeper" who was difficult to persuade, although this view was by no means universal. His appointment to the Section, however, is generally viewed as politicizing the Section leadership, a view reinforced by one attorney's recollection of Schoen going door-to-door in the office urging career attorneys to call their Senators to push for Reynolds's confirmation as Associate Attorney General (Interview with Section attorney).

In addition to the selection of his appointed staff, Reynolds was influential in the hiring of line staff. The Department of Justice had a history of hiring attorneys of high academic stature or relevant experience. Most initial hires came through the Attorney General's Honors Program, begun in 1954 to attract highly qualified law school graduates. Each Division had its own hiring committee to ensure that Division choices reflected overall Departmental standards. According to John MacCoon, a member of the Civil Rights Division Hiring Committee, under Reynolds the Committee was "pretty much displaced" and persons were hired who previously would not have been selected for interviews. "They did not have the academic nor, you know, interest in Civil Rights or any kind of background or academic standing that would have allowed them to have been hired in the past. . . . To get people of their ideological ilk, Reynolds and company had to suspend the honors program because they couldn't find their kind of people among those qualified in that way" (Interview with John MacCoon, 1994).

The departures in quick succession of experienced litigators provided the opportunity to bring in attorneys whose legal records and philosophies differed from those of the traditional civil rights attorney. Although some of the new hires were known to be active in Republican politics or had Administration connections, the primary goal seemed to be to replace departing attorneys with less zealous types, rather than with attorneys zealous in the pursuit of conservative ideals. There may not have been a litmus test to ensure ideological agreement, but there was an effort to select against the type of activist attorneys generally found in civil rights work. An experienced attorney who was hired during this period said, "I understood they were looking for—and I viewed myself as this—just matter-of-fact lawyers, not necessarily lawyers with a cause. . . . I was not a conservative, I was not a card-carrying Republican in fact, I did not vote for Mr. Reagan. . . . They were looking for people, you know, like coming from a New York law firm, as opposed to being a civil rights advocate" (Interview with Section attorney).

Despite the emphasis on avoiding traditional civil rights advocates, at least two attorneys with strong civil rights backgrounds and experience were hired in

Special Litigation during the Reagan Administration. One, who had worked in public interest law representing the disabled, was asked detailed questions by Deputy Assistant Disler during his interview about how he would handle disputes with Reynolds and his deputies (Interview with Section attorney). Another had extensive experience in disability issues and had even worked as an aide to Senator Edward Kennedy (D-Mass.), known for his liberal views on such matters. Although she had contacts and letters of support from a bipartisan assortment of legislators, she had tried unsuccessfully for several years to get into Special Litigation, believing that her path was blocked by well-meaning advocates within the Department who thought her background was too controversial to get past Reynolds. In exasperation, she tracked Reynolds down after a speech he gave at a stakeholder group meeting, followed him into an elevator as he was leaving, and presented him with her resumé, all the while relating the history of her efforts to get hired. Despite her clear record of advocacy, Reynolds hired her and she went on to develop one of the most constructive working relationships with him of any of the line attorneys, a relationship discussed in greater detail in Chapter 6 (Interview with Section attorney).

In addition to hiring attorneys who were clearly advocates, Reynolds was not as active as he could have been in removing attorneys who disagreed with him, unless they engaged in sabotage. Although his policies and manner led to the departure of many attorneys, he took no steps to engage in mass firings, reportedly leading to criticism from some Administration hard-liners that this was a sign of his ideological weakness (Interview with Section attorney). But another Section attorney, although acknowledging that Reynolds did not generally seek to fire people, stated that he believed the reason behind Reynolds's restraint was that removing attorneys "would have been seen as an attempt to undermine the work of the Section, a very high-risk strategy" (Interview with Section attorney).

Both supervisors and attorneys felt that there was a chronic shortage of attorneys in Special Litigation until about 1988, due both to delays in filling positions and reductions in authorized slots (Dinerstein, 1989; Interview with Arthur Peabody, 1994). The pool from which replacements could be selected grew smaller over time, and few had the high credentials previously associated with Justice attorneys. The attorneys hired through contacts or because of ideology were not of the same caliber as previous merit-based hires (Interview with John MacCoon, 1994).

CONCLUSION

William Bradford Reynolds took office with the clear goal to curtail the sort of civil rights enforcement that the Administration believed infringed upon the states' prerogative to conduct their own affairs, at least when that prerogative coincided with the Administration's own policy preference. With respect to CRIPA, that meant reducing the type of violations that were seen to implicate federal interests, and giving states wide latitude to formulate their own remedies and timetables. Reynolds sought to achieve this goal by limiting attorney discretion through review of pleadings, appointing like-minded deputies and assistants, increasing managerial oversight, requiring the involvement of the Bureau of Prisons in prison cases, and becoming personally involved in dealing with state officials and attorneys. In litigation, he was not constrained by positions that had been advanced by the Department of Justice under previous administrations, nor by prior alliances with other parties.

Section recommendations in litigation and investigations were not always followed, in many instances reflecting a departure from prior operations, but clear-cut policy statements were infrequent. Interventions were drastically curtailed, and the permissible scope of remedies was limited to constitutional minima under a narrow reading of a Supreme Court decision. Institutional litigation was rarely undertaken, with lengthy investigations defended as reflecting the negotiation and conciliation envisioned in CRIPA statutory language. If an institution was deemed to have constitutional deficiencies, the preferred way to address the problem was by a general consent decree that differed in specificity and remedies from those that the Department had historically negotiated. The Section was funded at a level that did not permit increased enforcement activity, and departed careerists were not always replaced. Those who were hired as replacements generally did not share the advocacy zeal of the attorneys who departed. The primary Section supervisors were kept in acting periods for lengthy periods, and in one case a supervisor was appointed with the expectation that he would limit enforcement activity. CRIPA enforcement during the Reagan Administration mirrors the increased managerial control imposed across the Administration, as well as the change in enforcement characteristic of the overall civil rights policy of the Administration.

• 5 •

Reaction from Without: Congress and Stakeholders

Reaction to an administrative strategy can come from two directions: internally, from careerists and appointees within the affected agency; or externally, from Congress, interest groups and other stakeholders, the judiciary, the media, and the public. The involvement of the judiciary and the media in CRIPA matters was as conduits for other actors, so they will not be discussed separately. Public involvement consisted primarily of congressional testimony, and other than a few parents who may have testified, there is no evidence of significant involvement outside of organized groups. The external reaction to the Reagan Administration's CRIPA policy is thus examined by reviewing how the two primary actors, Congress and stakeholders, sought to influence the continued pursuit of that policy.

CONGRESSIONAL REACTION TO CRIPA ENFORCEMENT

The 1980 election ushered in a Republican President as well as the first Republican Senate since 1954. In the wake of Reagan's long coattails, it was not surprising that it took a moderate Republican, Senator Lowell Weicker of Connecticut, to conduct the only significant Senate review of CRIPA activities. In the House, the most critical examinations were led by a sponsor of CRIPA, Representative Robert Kastenmeier (D-Wis.).

Authorization, Appropriation, and Oversight

Most congressional reviews of CRIPA enforcement came through the annual authorization and appropriation hearings, and these were lengthiest during Reagan's first term. Criticism of the Administration's overall civil rights enforcement began with the first Justice Department authorization hearing held after the new Administration took office, in February 1982 (*Authorization Request for the Civil Rights Division of the Department of Justice*, 1982; *Department of Justice Authorization for FY 83*, 1982). That hearing came on the heels of the issuance of a report by the Leadership Conference on Civil Rights, which stated that the Administration had essentially abandoned civil rights enforcement. Attorney General Smith called such claims "propaganda" and said that the Department was "enforcing the civil rights statutes to the fullest," promising to provide data to support his position (*Department of Justice Authorization for FY 83*, 1982, p. 28). With respect to CRIPA, the submission provided later by Reynolds contended that 16 new investigations had then been launched under CRIPA since its passage (p. 91), although the submission did not mention that 10 of the investigations had been started before Reagan took office and only one had been brought since Reynolds's confirmation. Reynolds also stated that 13 cases had "been the subject of significant court action since CRIPA was passed," but did not indicate that only one of those cases had been initiated during the Reagan Administration. The submission also said that "just last week one state decided to close a clearly sub-par institution following our initial investigation" (p. 91), which although true, implied a causal connection that was undocumented.

The type of criticism leveled at the Department and the detailed paperwork that Congress required to be submitted sent a clear message to the Administration that data would be needed to support its contention that "in the past year the level of government activity has been at an all-time high" (*Authorization Request for the Civil Rights Division of the Department of Justice*, 1982 (p. 415). The closing comments of Representative Don Edwards (D-Cal.), like Kastenmeier a sponsor of CRIPA, show the level of discourse that characterized that hearing:

It seems to me that the thread that runs through your testimony and statement is that on all these issues you know better than anyone else. You know better than the Supreme Court how to interpret the Constitution. You know better than the district court judges who have listened to evidence in a case for months or years what the proper remedies are. . . . You lecture civil rights groups about what they should do to advance the interests of their members. Yet, you have been here less than a year, and you have come to us with very little experience in civil rights. (pp. 337–338)

Representative Edwards went on to urge Reynolds to heed career Justice attorneys who "have strong reservations about this radical course that you have embarked upon."

The next major hearing involving CRIPA came about as part of an oversight hearing on Section 504 of the Rehabilitation Act (*Enforcement of Section 504 of the Rehabilitation Act*, 1983). This hearing, led by Senator Weicker, father of a child with mental disabilities and a well-known advocate for the disabled, took place after the much-publicized resignation of Special Litigation attorney Timothy Cook. The focus of the hearing, according to Weicker, was to "examine charges that DOJ has retreated from its role as defender of the rights of the mentally retarded in institutions" and to "send a clear signal to the DOJ, the States, and the American people that the rights of mentally retarded individuals in institutions will be protected" (p. 2).

In his opening statement, Reynolds downplayed reliance upon the number of lawsuits to indicate enforcement activity, stating that the "measure of success is not how many lawsuits are brought, but how many constitutionally intolerable situations have been remedied" (p. 5). He told the Subcommittee that CRIPA's statutory language reflects congressional intent to avoid litigation. "The genius of the bipartisan congressional approach is that it offers a way to get this job done with the absolute minimum of State-Federal legal confrontation."

Reynolds was asked detailed questions about his interpretation of the *Youngberg* case and about the departures of several Section attorneys. He stated that the resignations were the result of philosophical differences about what the Constitution and federal law allow the government to remedy. The most acrimonious exchange took place in a discussion about the closing line of a letter detailing deficiencies found during a CRIPA investigation, which said, "We are available and willing to discuss [these deficiencies] at your convenience" (p. 43). Weicker grilled Reynolds about the use of the phrase "at your convenience": Weicker: "Mr. Attorney General, you can move in on a situation like that tomorrow. Now, let us not sit and play games." Reynolds: "Senator, I do not play games in this area, and I do not think this is a game playing area." Weicker: "Pretty please, do not rape my daughter? Pretty please, do not go ahead and beat my son?"(pp. 44–45).

Weicker also questioned whether it is appropriate for the government to rely on the remediation efforts of the very states that created the problems. Reynolds said that the Administration would "ride herd on the States," and would make sure that they act (p. 51). The hearing ended with Weicker stating that he would ask the subcommittee to direct its staff to go into the field, visit institutions, and prepare a report on their findings.

A hearing in the House on CRIPA enforcement, led by Representatives Edwards and Kastenmeier, took place around the same time and covered similar ground (*Civil Rights of Institutionalized Persons Act Hearing*, 1983, 1984). Efforts by witnesses, including former Section attorneys, to generate uniform congressional outrage were unsuccessful, and an observation by Representative Thomas DeWine (R-Oh.) about the tremendous amount of prosecutorial discretion in CRIPA typified the prevailing attitude. This remark echoed Reynolds's oft-stated position that the Department was enforcing CRIPA in accordance with congressional intent. Some representatives, however, agreed with witnesses that the lack of specificity in CRIPA made it easy for the Administration to always take the most lenient view toward states in investigations. Representative Patricia Schroeder (D-Col.), in a question to a former careerist who was testifying, criticized Reynolds's reliance on discretionary language, implying that he was being somewhat devious: "What you are saying is the loophole isn't so big you could drive a truck through, but it is big enough for a snake to get through," to which career employee Timothy Cook replied, "I think that is an apt analogy" (p. 76).

The subcommittee report instigated by Senator Weicker was examined in a hearing about 18 months later (*Care of Institutionalized Mentally Disabled Persons*, 1985). That subcommittee also heard from private attorneys and parents about the slow pace of investigations and the lack of interest they experienced in their encounters with Justice attorneys. The staff's report was critical, detailing the length of investigations and the lack of specificity in remedial language. But, despite the overwhelmingly negative tone of the report, its conclusions were tempered. "The Department's conciliatory approach in this case and others has the *potential* to negate the type of federal involvement in basic health and safety issues envisioned and mandated in CRIPA" (p. 169), and "although the arguments presented by the DOJ *do not appear* to directly contradict the Supreme Court's holding in *Youngberg*, they are a restrictive interpretation of the case and one which is contrary to arguments presented by commentators and several recent judicial interpretations" (p. 245). For his part, in that hearing Reynolds continued to rely on the conciliation language in CRIPA, emphasizing actions that had been taken in various cases, and claiming "a solid record of action under CRIPA" (p. 410).

As had previously been the case, a House subcommittee also held a hearing the same week the Senate hearing began, but this was on all aspects of civil rights enforcement (*Authorization Request for the Civil Rights Division*, 1985). With respect to CRIPA, in this hearing Reynolds said, "Our understanding of the statute was discussed at some length during last year's hearings. While there appears to be some disagreement, we have been offered no reasoned basis to depart from our present course under CRIPA, a course that coincides fully with the intent of Congress" (p. 270).

The Senate subcommittee's staff report and the hearings on Reynolds's nomination to become Associate Attorney General reveal much detail about the Administration's early CRIPA enforcement. After 1985, congressional interest in CRIPA waned and hearings became less involved and confrontational. Persons who had testified previously had little new information to offer because they were no longer in the Department, and there were no major changes in the Administration's efforts. The 1986 authorization hearing is noteworthy only for the lack of congressional interest (*Authorization Request for the Civil Rights Division*, 1986). Reynolds, having little to lose at that point, took the offensive, observing that it was the fifth time he had been up for an authorization hearing, and that they always opened with a comment that the Administration is retreating on civil rights. "When all of that rhetoric is said and done, at the end of each of the hearings and the facts are in the record which we put in the record, it seems invariably to be the case that the facts overwhelm the rhetoric" (p. 3). No representative seriously challenged this statement.

Congressional criticism of CRIPA enforcement became muted. In 1987, Senator Orrin Hatch (R-Ut.), a sponsor of CRIPA, commended the Administration for the change in institutional conditions that he said investigations had produced, and went on to say that the Administration "had admirably inaugurated the enforcement" of CRIPA (*Authorization, Legislation and Oversight of the U.S. Department of Justice*, 1987, p. 7). In that hearing, as well as in that same year's authorization hearing (*Authorization Request for the Civil Rights Division*, 1987), Reynolds submitted a compilation of the Division's activities during the entire Reagan Administration. In neither of these hearings were substantive questions asked about CRIPA.

The final major congressional hearing to address CRIPA enforcement came in 1988 before the Senate (*Department of Justice Authorization for FY 1989*, 1988). Senator Edward Kennedy opened with the statement that Attorney General Meese's recent appointment of Reynolds as "Counselor to the Attorney General" amounted to an "end run around the Senate" (p. 122), in reference to the Senate's earlier failure to approve Reynolds's nomination to be Associate Attorney General. Despite the late date, Reynolds's response was not conciliatory:

I must say, I have sat here and listened again to the same sort of shopworn speeches that have been delivered all too repetitively in the last 7 years, and as usual, the polarizing rhetoric is one that takes little account at all of the actual record of the civil rights enforcement compiled by this administration during the 1980's, a record that showed unprecedented enforcement activity in all phases of Federal responsibility, from the number of investigations commenced to the number of lawsuits brought challenging discriminatory conduct, to the successes achieved, to the number of victims able to assert that the wrongs against them have been righted. (p. 125)

Although Reynolds was referring to the entire spectrum of civil rights enforcement in the above statement, his tone was the same when he talked explicitly about CRIPA:

In 1980, at the time Pres. Reagan was first elected to office, there was a new and as yet untried statute in the Federal code, the Civil Rights of Institutionalized Persons Act or CRIPA. During this decade of the eighties, that statute has been vigorously enforced by the Civil Rights Division to correct egregious and flagrant unconstitutional conditions. . . . This extraordinary record has been accomplished with a minimum amount of litigation so as to maximize cooperation at the State and local levels and ensure that the State's scarce resources will be available for use in improving the deplorable conditions at these facilities at the earliest practical time. This remarkable record of accomplishments, which is fully documented in materials made available to this committee not only today but over the past 7 years, puts the lie to those bombastic assertions that we have turned back the civil rights clock, or been inattentive to our law enforcement responsibilities in this vital area. (p. 151)

Reynolds defended the tenor of his remarks, stating that polarization was necessary and proper, and that his language was the same sort used by Senators Kennedy and Metzenbaum at the onset of the hearing (p. 151).

When asked in an interview about his experience with congressional hearings, Reynolds criticized congressional motives and authority:

I think that Congress has no business . . . Congress's oversight hearings are a joke. They have no authority to do them, they shouldn't be doing them, the legislative branch is operating in an arena it is not authorized to operate . . . . I think it was the case that Cook [attorney Timothy Cook] and others in this area . . . convinced certainly Weicker, who was very interested in this area because he has a kid, that we were undermining everything that was important for disability rights, not just institutionalized persons. And Weicker's view was, ok, we got to get him out of there. We've either got to get him out of there or we've got to so neutralize him that he won't know what he's doing. And how do we do it? We embarrass him with public hearings. . . . So I perceived it to be, and I still to this day think it was, a game. They were holding hearings not because they ever intended to amend the statute, not because they had any interest in amending the statute, but in order to try to either bring me back to where I'd say yes, I'll do whatever Cook says, or to have such a hew and cry generated around this issue that the President says, gee, we gotta get rid of this guy because he's distracting others. And that's basically the game plan for oversight hearings, that's why they have them. . . . (Interview with William Bradford Reynolds, 1993)

Although Reynolds outlasted his congressional critics, on one issue—his nomination to be Associate Attorney General—there was an opportunity to publicly rebuff him, and it proved to be a confirmation hearing exceeded recently in contentiousness perhaps only by hearings on Supreme Court nominations.

Confirmation Hearings

Three persons active in the Administration's CRIPA enforcement, Deputy Assistants J. Harvie Wilkinson, III, and Charles Cooper, as well as Assistant Attorney General Reynolds, were rewarded by the President for their overall efforts with nominations to other posts. At each of their confirmation hearings, the Senate had ample opportunity to critique CRIPA policy.

William Bradford Reynolds

Reynolds's first encounter with the Senate came at his confirmation hearing for the Assistant Attorney General position (*Department of Justice Confirmations*, 1981). He stated the view on CRIPA that he would adhere to consistently: that the primary responsibility to remedy institutional conditions is with states, which should be given the opportunity to institute voluntary remedial action. Only after every effort to seek such remedial action has failed is litigation warranted, and then remedies should be consistent with the Constitution with specific details left to the states.

Reynolds was very clear about his approach, and the Judiciary Committee members were not especially critical of his position. In fact, one Senator questioned whether Reynolds could really effect change in the established Department of Justice bureaucracy:

Are we going to have the same people who were there before, the same people, the same group, the same politics, the same attitudes? Is it going to be business as usual? Are we going to have a lot of the Carter holdovers there who will simply remain entrenched, hunker down, let the political top turn, a new President, new Senators, new Congressmen, new this and that but the bureaucracy will hunker down and nothing will change? (pp. 134–135, comments of Sen. James East (R-N.C.))

Reynolds easily won confirmation, and Senator East's remarks provided congressional support for his efforts to change policy direction.

In 1985, Reynolds was nominated to be the Associate Attorney General of the United States, the third-ranking position in the Department of Justice. Even before the confirmation hearing began, critics were calling on the Senate to reject the nomination (*Reynolds Nomination*, 1985). Reynolds and his supporters expected a tough fight focusing primarily on the Administration's efforts to amend consent decrees in employment discrimination cases so as to eliminate quotas as remedies (Williams, 1985). No doubt mindful of the expectation that Reynolds would staunchly defend his record on the controversial issues of busing and quotas, Judiciary Committee opponents, led by Senator Joseph Biden (D-Del.), focused on the more technical and less publicized areas of voting rights and CRIPA enforcement (*Nomination of William Bradford Reynolds*, 1985).

In opening statements, Senator Kennedy referred to "4 years of nullification" of CRIPA by Reynolds (p. 4), and Senator Metzenbaum stated, "If this is indeed an administration that believes that the law should be enforced, then that means all laws, not just those that somebody in the Department thinks should be enforced" (p. 8). Reynolds, in response to sympathetic questioning from Senator Hatch, called his CRIPA enforcement "truly remarkable" and again pointed to the procedural requirements and negotiation language contained in the statute. Hatch stated that he had written those procedural approaches "so that the States would not feel like they were being dumped on by the Justice Department" (p. 36). To illustrate that Reynolds was not an Administration renegade, the submissions supporting the nomination included a letter from Attorney General Smith assuring the Committee that the policies Reynolds pursued were the policies of the President (p. 45), and Reynolds added that he kept the Attorney General informed of his activities through weekly staff meetings.

Opponents, mainly former careerists, stakeholders, and persons involved in institutional litigation, covered some of the same ground reviewed in oversight hearings and the Senate subcommittee report. In addition to what they characterized as a restrictive interpretation of CRIPA and case law, opponents accused Reynolds of indifference to the plight of the institutionalized and of failing to appreciate the scope of problems. To illustrate, one stakeholder group report referred to a comment Reynolds made in 1982 in which he claimed, "Rarely does one find today the kind of blatant, inhumane brutalization of inmates that stands out like a constitutional red flag to even the most casual observer" (Washington Council of Lawyers, 1983, p. 691). The report stated that such minimization of institutional problems makes it easier to "justify reduced levels of activity and attention" (p. 694).

This confirmation hearing was the climax of concerted, detailed opposition by former careerists and stakeholders to the Administration's CRIPA implementation, yet the testimony most damaging to Reynolds did not relate directly to enforcement. Senator Paul Simon (D-Ill.) asked Reynolds whether the high turnover in the Special Litigation Section was due to disagreement with

Reynolds's position on CRIPA enforcement, and Reynolds's response rejected that notion:

I have no knowledge that that is the case, Senator. I do know that there has been a turn-over within the Civil Rights Division. I think that in that section, there has been quite a large turnover. But the people who have left have left at different times throughout the 4 years, and that is not unusual—indeed, the same kind of a phenomenon goes on yearly in the Department in all the divisions—lawyers come; they stay for a time; if there are other opportunities that they are interested in, they move on. And I believe that has been the process that has worked. I do not personally know what motivated any lawyer to leave the Department in any section. . . . I know of only one lawyer that I think properly and accurately would fit into that category. (pp. 132–133)

This line of questioning was perhaps unanticipated by Reynolds and his staff. After Reynolds's initial testimony, a number of affidavits were submitted by former Special Litigation attorneys who stated they had left because of pol-icy disagreements known to Reynolds. A third day of hearings was scheduled to examine, in the words of Senator Metzenbaum, "Whether Mr. Reynolds delib-erately made falsehoods or whether he forgot something or omitted something or cares to explain his statements" (p. 845). Reynolds backtracked: "I did not regard any of them as doing a resignation under protest. They all had other jobs. They were all going to other places from the Division. But they did indeed in the exit interviews express to me that disagreement" (p. 931).

Reynolds went on to say that he thought Senator Simon had been asking about whether there had been mass resignations in protest, and that he had an-swered no because there had not been any. A compilation of attorney turnover submitted by Reynolds to the Committee listed numbers for the Division as a whole, and did not single out the Special Litigation Section, the focus of the specific questions.

A confirmation hearing that was expected to focus on busing and quotas, is-sues on which Reynolds felt comfortable defending his record, instead resulted in efforts by senators who opposed the nomination to paint Reynolds as evasive and less than truthful in answering questions about attorney departures and voting rights. One commentator suggested that opponents had shied away from busing and quotas because those were known to be unpopular issues (Brownstein, 1985). The lesser issues became an easier way to oppose a nomi-nee whom some believed was not going to be confirmed by the committee in any event (Interview with Section attorney).

The Judiciary Committee voted 10–8 against approving the Reynolds nomination and sending it on to the Senate floor, and tied 9–9 on a motion to send the nomination to the floor without a recommendation, with the tie vote defeating the motion. Although the nomination was defeated, some analysts did not interpret the vote as a referendum on overall civil rights enforcement because so much of the debate had focused on the least controversial issues (Brownstein, 1985).

Reynolds and his defenders viewed the defeat of his nomination as the result of an unfair attack on his character, rather than a debate on his policies (Kmiec, 1992; Wolfson, 1986). One supporter said the vote illustrated that Reynolds was "too intellectually honest to be promoted" (Kmiec, 1992, p. 162). Reynolds remains bitter about the confirmation hearing:

Biden couldn't come out and say, this guy is a disaster because he's against busing and quotas. Because he knew as well as I knew that the majority of the people outside the Beltway, black and white, were against busing and quotas. He couldn't come out and say, "Jeez, we gotta get after this guy because of his response to *Stotts*," because the Supreme Court said what it said in *Stotts*. That's why when you come out and hang yourself on the Supreme Court, they suddenly have a problem. So what they did is they picked Voting Rights Act and CRIPA and they sort of tried to, and with some success obviously, manufacture through those areas that I was dissembling or I was doing something that I shouldn't do in those areas that was not carrying out the law. And then they would sprinkle here and there the quota issue, but they didn't want it to be centerpiece and they couldn't afford to because they knew that politically, I'd win. . . . I don't even think that was a secret. Biden has said that he had sat down with his people, and with Ralph Neas and the people at the Leadership Conference, and had told them flat out, we got to find an issue outside of the ones that are really the bones of contention. He did the Louisiana redistricting, he did a very dishonest job on it, but he did a heck of a job, and that was one of the things that he used as an excuse to get me. And Specter again, he used Voting Rights Act, this idea that somehow I'd misled him five years ago in another hearing. But CRIPA was a tool, it was available to them and was something that, if they came out and said, Jeez, I was out there disregarding and not paying attention to all these people who were being treated like something worse than you can imagine in these institutions, everybody would say they were shocked, and we can't vote for him. (Interview with William Bradford Reynolds, 1993)

Although Reynolds was handed a setback in the defeat of his nomination, it seemed only to reinforce his commitment to pursue his course of civil rights enforcement. His apparent resolve was depicted dramatically by a sympathetic writer: "Reynolds was to remain as Assistant Attorney General of the Civil Rights Division. He was stoic in defeat. Turning to his associate, Charles Cooper, he said, 'Let's go. We have a division to run' " (Wolfson, 1986, p. 62).

As events transpired, instead of just the Division, Reynolds had a Department to run. Although retaining his title as Assistant Attorney General, he was also named Counselor to the Attorney General, taking over many of the duties he would have had as Associate Attorney General had he been confirmed. The nomination defeat made little immediate difference, although in the long run it essentially removed Reynolds from being considered for other positions requiring Senate confirmation.

The other Civil Rights Division officials who received nominations were ultimately confirmed, but both also faced unusual scrutiny given the level of their appointments.

J. Harvie Wilkinson, III

J. Harvie Wilkinson, III, was appointed a Deputy Assistant Attorney General in the summer of 1982, and was given oversight responsibility for Special Litigation. With respect to CRIPA enforcement, he received mixed reviews, being credited with facilitating the appointments of career attorneys as Section Chief and Deputy Section Chief (Interview with John MacCoon, 1994; Interview with Arthur Peabody, 1994), but receiving criticism for taking limited and uninformed positions in civil rights enforcement.

In August 1983, after a relatively brief stint at Justice, Wilkinson was nominated to fill a vacancy on the United States Court of Appeals for the Fourth Circuit, bypassing the lower district court rung in an unusual career progression for someone with no judicial or even trial experience. The nomination was viewed as a reflection of Wilkinson's connections and his loyalty to the Administration's policy preferences (Antonelli, 1984). Wilkinson's confirmation hearing had to be postponed and rescheduled due to the number of people who wanted to testify (*Confirmation Hearings on Federal Appointments*, 1983). When the hearing finally took place, CRIPA enforcement was not an issue. Opposition to the nomination came primarily from civil rights groups who felt that the nomination of someone with so little experience illustrated the good-old-boy network at its worst (*Confirmation Hearings on Federal Appointments*, 1984). Wilkinson was confirmed, and currently sits on the Fourth Circuit. Because of his position, he declined a request to be interviewed.

Charles J. Cooper

Charles J. Cooper came to the Justice Department as a Special Assistant to Reynolds, and later was named to be a Deputy Assistant Attorney General. After Wilkinson's departure, Cooper was given oversight responsibility for Special Litigation. In 1985, after Reynolds's nomination had been rejected, a hearing was held on Cooper's nomination to head the Office of Legal Counsel (*Confirmation Hearings on Federal Appointments*, 1985). Although not nearly as detailed or confrontational as the Reynolds hearing, the Cooper hearing was contentious, especially for a nomination that typically attracts little attention.

Senator Simon referred to a report prepared by his staff that stated that Cooper had "substantially restricted the civil rights of institutionalized persons, both prisoners and the handicapped" (p. 580). Cooper repeated the Administration's position that the language of CRIPA precluded more aggressive or far-reaching enforcement. He also delineated his responsibility for reviewing CRIPA actions to the period during which he served as a Deputy, although attorneys in Special Litigation frequently refer to Cooper's involvement in CRIPA matters during the period he was a Special Assistant. This delineation allowed Cooper to avoid the specific questions on turnover that had plagued Reynolds, for Cooper could say that most of the substantial turnover occurred before he became a Deputy. Cooper also took pains to praise the work of the Special Litigation Section: "I think my work in supervising that section has presented me, personally, with more self-satisfaction, with a greater sense of rewards, psychic rewards, knowing the kind of, really, the unspeakable conditions that some of these institutions are, are in, and expose their residents to, that we can bring relief, and bring it about as quickly as possible" (p. 581).

Although Cooper won confirmation to head the Office of Legal Counsel, he felt he was asked for more information and reviewed more carefully than were any other comparable nominees:

If you compare me to Brad, then yes, I got off easy. If you compare me to anyone else, including for example, . . . the guy going in to the Solicitor General's job, Charles Fried, all of them, we were all in the same space of time. Richard Willard, Charles Fried, John Bolton . . . if you compare me to any of them, I didn't have that easy of a time. They, the committee, not only asked for that list of cases, but they researched this. They asked for every document that had a, you know, a Cooper fingerprint on it. And we just gave up reams and reams of documents. (Interview with Charles Cooper, 1993)

The attention paid to the Administration's CRIPA enforcement, and the information and detail required in the various confirmation hearings, seemed only to reinforce the Administration's view that its approach was sound. But other than revealing a need for documentation, the hearings resulted in little change in CRIPA policy preference and the level of enforcement. Section attorneys who provided information to congressional committees expressed disappointment in the staffs' understanding of issues, as well as the lack of any real impact of congressional activity on the Administration's enforcement. One attorney who said he had a "story to tell" waited in vain for an invitation to testify, despite his having provided information to a committee in the course of its investigation. In recalling his frustration, he said: "I think I was really naive about Congress because for me it was such a big decision to tell anyone about any of this. . . . I really struggled with it. It was really hard for me. . . . And when I saw [a representative] lying, and that most of the committee members had no interest in this at all, although to me it was just so outrageous, I realized that this avenue was a total waste. . . . It's a bunch of jaded clowns" (Interview with Section attorney). Another Section attorney states that he believes the careerists were used by Congress: "They really thought they were being heroes, but these Congressmen were not going to do anything for these people" (Interview with Section attorney).

No serious efforts to amend CRIPA were undertaken as a result of the hearings previously discussed. The only bills pertaining to CRIPA introduced during the Reagan Administration, S. 1540 (1987) and H.R. 3033 (1987), were designed to require the notification and permit the involvement of Protection and Advocacy (P&A) groups in CRIPA litigation. Attention to this area came about as a result of intervention efforts by P&A groups in CRIPA lawsuits in Connecticut, Massachusetts, and Oregon. These bills died in committee, and CRIPA was not amended. A Section attorney summarized his view of congressional activity by saying that he believed CRIPA amendments were never seriously considered because they would have faced almost certain veto, so the only tools available to Congress were "public indignation" and "embarrassing the executive" (Interview with Section attorney).

The role of Congress in affecting the Administration's administrative strategy in CRIPA implementation was therefore very limited, serving primarily to illustrate the need for the Administration to document its claims of activity and foreclose the Administration's effort to formally reward Reynolds for his loyal service. In light of the public record and the reported unwillingness of congressional staff to pursue information provided by careerists, it appears that Reynolds is correct in his observation that congressional oversight was driven more by personal political animosity than by substantive CRIPA policy disagreement. Political appointees applying an administrative strategy to achieve policy preferences unpopular with Congress would do well to take a lesson from Reynolds and stand firm in the face of criticism, waiting for Congress to act. In the case of CRIPA, Reynolds called the congressional bluff.

STAKEHOLDER REACTION TO CRIPA ENFORCEMENT

Department of Justice institutional enforcement activity had for many years been dependent on the existence of stakeholder-sponsored litigation, and careerists expected that stakeholders would provide the details of institutional conditions necessary to support the launching of CRIPA investigations. With the change in the Administration and indications of a shift in enforcement philosophy, Section attorneys reported that they found it increasingly difficult to obtain information from stakeholders, who often were distrustful of what Justice would do. Further, as experienced attorneys left the Department of Justice, they were replaced by attorneys who lacked stakeholder contacts, and even known contacts hesitated to cooperate with unknown quantities. One Section attorney related how he had to be vouched for by a departing attorney before members of a stakeholder group would agree to talk to him. This diminution of intelligence-gathering capacity was accompanied by stakeholder activity directed against Administration enforcement on two fronts—public exposure and criticism, and litigation.

Statements, Testimony, and Publications

The first stakeholder report on civil rights enforcement, including CRIPA implementation, set the pattern of trying to put the Reagan Administration on the defensive. *Without Justice* was issued in 1982 by the Leadership Conference on Civil Rights, an organization established in 1950 and consisting of more than 160 civil rights groups. The report criticized civil rights enforcement across the board, and was heavily relied upon by Congress in its 1982 hearings, even being appended to the record of one (*Department of Justice Authorization for FY 83*, 1982). An attorney who provided information to the Senate Judiciary Committee during the confirmation hearings on Reynolds's nomination to be Associate Attorney General stated that the Leadership Conference coordinated the testimony of witnesses in that the hearing, and that group bore the primary responsibility for the nomination's defeat (Interview with Section attorney).

Shortly after the Leadership Conference report was issued, the Washington Council of Lawyers, a voluntary bar association, issued its own review of civil rights enforcement during the first twenty months of the Reagan Administration, and this was also a critical document (Washington Council of Lawyers, 1983). Similarly, the ACLU issued its detailed, negative assessment of all aspects of civil rights enforcement (American Civil Liberties Union, 1984). These reports contained evaluations of CRIPA enforcement as part of overall examinations of administrative activity. Such groups as the NAACP Legal Defense Fund and the National Lawyers Guild made only passing reference to CRIPA in their more broad-range indictments of civil rights activity. Another group, the Committee for Public Justice, focused its written criticism on CRIPA activity, but did little more than summarize congressional testimony (Gordon, 1986).

CRIPA enforcement was the primary focus of concern for certain stakeholders, especially those groups dealing with the rights of persons with mental disabilities. In early 1983, a coalition of 22 public interest, civil rights, and professional organizations joined the director of the Mental Health Law Project in writing a letter to Reynolds accusing him of abandoning the Justice Department's statutory obligation to the mentally retarded (Civil rights of institutionalized persons act, 1983). This outcry was prompted by the leaking of Reynolds's June 1982 memo interpreting *Youngberg v. Romeo*. Reynolds responded quickly to the charge, welcoming the writers' concern but stating that their view "misapprehends the depth of commitment and the extent of activity of the Civil Rights Division in enforcing the Civil Rights of Institutionalized Persons Act" (Reynolds, 1983, January 17, p. 1). In his letter, Reynolds invited the director of the Mental Health Law Project and other representatives to meet with him to discuss the issue. He included with his response a copy of remarks he had made two months earlier before the American Bar Association's Commission on the Mentally Disabled.

The editors of the *Mental Disability Law Reporter*, the publication of the Mental Health Law Project, examined the correspondence and the entire disagreement, and concluded that the Administration's approach to CRIPA was "not without support in the legislative history," but that Reynolds's interpretation of *Youngberg* was not as well-founded (Civil rights of institutionalized persons act, 1983, p. 8). The editors called upon Reynolds to broaden his review by incorporating caselaw and statutory analyses, with the hope that the conclusion he would then reach would have broader support from those interested in protecting the civil rights of persons with disabilities. The group's initial adversarial posture seemed tempered by the fact that Reynolds had responded quickly and calmly to their criticism, provided a legal basis for his opinion, and invited critics to meet with him.

A more embarrassing criticism of the Administration's policies came from the Reagan-appointed President's Committee on Mental Retardation. In 1984, the Committee adopted a resolution condemning the position Justice had taken in a brief filed in the Supreme Court, in which Justice argued against the existence of the right of retarded persons in a state's care to live in the environment which is least restrictive (of liberty). Although the Department's brief was not filed in a case arising under CRIPA, it reflected the Administration's view that the constitutional rights of institutionalized persons should be defined narrowly. The Committee's resolution was inserted in the Congressional Record by Senator Weicker (President's Committee on Mental Retardation, 1984, June 11), but the criticized brief was not withdrawn by Justice. It was difficult during this period for stakeholders supporting the notion of housing in a least restrictive environment and community placements to make much headway, because they frequently faced opposition from parents who opposed the deinstitutionalization of their children. Several of these parents' groups were represented by Washington attorney Joel Klein, who had opposed Justice in institutional litigation under previous administrations but who had more policy opinions in common with Reynolds and frequently met with him (Interview with Arthur Peabody, 1994).

Stakeholders interested in mental disability issues received more coverage and attention from Congress and the Administration than did those concerned with prisoners' rights. Only one such organization, the National Prison Project of the ACLU, actively publicized its disagreement with CRIPA enforcement (Alexander, 1984). The main thrust of its efforts, however, came in litigation.

There was a steady undercurrent of activity by stakeholders to gain access to Reynolds, and to attempt to educate him in accordance with their views. He was invited by many stakeholder groups to attend meetings and to speak before them, and he accepted a number of invitations. His willingness to confront attackers was a deliberate strategy to quiet criticism:

The people who were effective were people like Pendleton—Penny was wonderful—Clarence Thomas, I think myself, who were willing to say, yeah, this is what we believe. And we were willing to go into the lion's den and say it. I mean, I went into Harlem, I went into all of those places, and stood up and said, hey, this is why I believe. . . . And if you articulate what you believe, and give a reasoned basis for it, your opportunity to kind of at least hold back the tide, if not make inroads, is a lot greater. (Interview with William Bradford Reynolds, 1993)

Reynolds's willingness to meet with his critics and discuss issues occasionally resulted in his adopting a more expansive view of civil rights than he would normally be expected to have. In one instance detailed by a career attorney, Reynolds was persuaded by an expert and the attorney to take a controversial stance against the use of aversive treatment in institutions, specifically behavior modification techniques using electroshock. He agreed to language in a consent decree calling the use of such methods an unconstitutional restraint, and maintained this position in the face of opposition from such mainstream organizations as the American Psychological Association (Interview with Section attorney).

Although stakeholders, especially those that had issued detailed reports, participated in and likely helped to instigate congressional inquiry, their attention-getting activities diminished following the denial of Reynolds's nomination to be Associate Attorney General. Litigation then became their tool of choice in efforts to influence policy.

Litigation

Prior to the Reagan Administration, the Justice Department and civil rights stakeholders had a synergistic litigation relationship. The stakeholders often provided the factual bases for lawsuits and identified representative plaintiffs, while the Justice Department contributed financial resources and technical expertise. Reynolds took a different view of what the relationship should be:

When I walked in there, it was the first time that the people who operated in that Division had to answer to anybody for what they did, and you know, I'm not disparaging Drew Days. I think he's a very intelligent guy and I think he's got a lot of strengths, but Drew Days was essentially willing to sign off on anything that was put in front of his nose, because that was the direction that everything was going. It was sort of . . . we, the Division, represent the groups, and that our constituency are the institutionalized persons and the minorities, and so we do what they say. And there was a backroom sort of process, if you will, that was very well-recognized and known. That the Legal Defense Fund, the NAACP, was signing off on things before we would put them out there. And if they didn't like the way it was written, they'd massage it. And you had people in the institutional, with the prison cases . . . that were representing the inmates were, holy cow, this Texas case with Judge Justice [*Ruiz v. Estelle*], they were running my crew—I really had to pull in some reins on that one. (Interview with William Bradford Reynolds, 1993)

"Pull in some reins" meant, in several cases, changing positions that the Justice Department had previously advocated in concurrence with stakeholder litigants. Although some Justice Department attorneys continued to do what they could behind the scenes to assist private plaintiffs, litigation strategies suddenly changed. Stakeholders with a history of working cooperatively with Justice began to oppose Justice involvement. As one former Special Litigation attorney who left to work for a stakeholder group stated: "We hope that the Reagan Justice Department doesn't use the Institutionalized Persons Act. The way it's being used, CRIPA has become a detriment to prisoner's rights" (Plotkin et al., 1989, p. 420, quoting Adjoa Aieyotoro of the National Prison Project).

Because stakeholders felt the scope of remedies sought by Reynolds was usually too limited, many took steps to formally participate in CRIPA litigation, arguing that the interests of the institutionalized were not being adequately represented by Justice. These efforts took the form of intervening in settlements "in order to disturb them, change them, modify them" (Interview with Arthur Peabody, 1994). The first and most bitter example of intervention by a stakeholder took place in the Michigan prison litigation. While Justice and the State of Michigan were negotiating the terms of the proposed consent decree, the Michigan Civil Liberties Union Foundation and the ACLU's National Prison Project filed a motion to be *amicus curiae* in the pending litigation. Additionally, inmate plaintiffs in a separate Michigan prison suit filed a motion to intervene. Both motions were granted, and these parties acted as vigorous opponents of and watchdogs over the Justice Department's efforts to submit a limited consent decree and to monitor that decree (*United States v. Michigan*,

1987). According to one of the National Prison Project attorneys, the consent decree that was ultimately adopted was enforced almost solely through that group's efforts (Plotkin, et al., 1989).

The Department established a precedent in the Michigan case to oppose stakeholder efforts to intervene as of right (mandatory intervention), as well as to oppose motions for permissive intervention in general. The Department's position was not surprising, for agreeing to mandatory intervention would mean agreeing with the finding that a court must make to grant such a motion—that Justice could not adequately represent the interests of those in the institution.

In mental health/mental retardation cases, stakeholders sought to participate primarily in order to promote community placement of the institutionalized as a prospective remedy. Intervention was sought by residents represented by the Mental Health Law Project in *United States v. Massachusetts*, and the court allowed the Project's participation as *amicus curiae*. The Project also represented residents of an Oregon mental retardation facility, who were ultimately permitted to intervene as of right when the U.S. Court of Appeals for the Ninth Circuit reversed the lower court's denial of the intervention request (*United States v. Oregon*). The Department's position in that case was tempered by the persuasive talent of a Special Litigation attorney who convinced Reynolds not to oppose permissive intervention, despite what she characterized as a "scathing, scathing" motion filed by the Mental Health Law Project (Interview with Section attorney). That same attorney was instrumental in preventing a Justice appeal of the Ninth Circuit's decision.

The last lawsuit filed by the Reagan Administration that precipitated significant stakeholder opposition concerned the Southbury Training School in Connecticut. The state Protection and Advocacy office, an agency established pursuant to federal law with the mission of protecting the interest of persons with disabilities, filed a motion to compel the State and Justice to include it in consent decree negotiations. The court rejected the request (*United States v. Connecticut*, 1986; Dinerstein, 1989). The battle with Connecticut's Protection and Advocacy office prompted the previously-discussed unsuccessful attempt to amend CRIPA so as to require notification of and consultation with such offices when institutions within their states became the target of Justice investigation. The Department's antagonism toward the involvement of stakeholders, at least in litigation, coupled with the departure of career Justice attorneys, "left a major gap in the section's institutional knowledge and memory" (Dinerstein, 1989, p. 407).

Although stakeholders adopted litigation as a way to oppose Justice efforts, the level of their litigation activity "declined substantially" over the term of the Reagan Administration (Interview with Arthur Peabody, 1994). The switch by

Justice from ally to adversary undoubtedly limited the ability of stakeholders to promote their own litigation, having fewer resources with which to fight more battles. The litigation strategy was more costly and had a narrower focus than did stakeholder efforts to affect policy through publications or congressional testimony, but it had a greater effect on institutional conditions because it went directly to the remedies a court could impose in a particular case. Ultimately, however, there is little indication that even the litigation strategy did much to alter the overall policy toward CRIPA, other than perhaps strengthening administrative resolve to avoid stakeholder involvement in litigation whenever possible.

CONCLUSION

The effect of the two primary external actors (Congress and stakeholders) on the Administration's CRIPA strategy was narrow and slight. The nature of congressional activity was more personal than policy-driven, with the greatest impact being the pressure that congressional hearings put on the Administration to document its enforcement record. Although Reynolds withstood the various hearings and survived for the entire period of the Administration, even increasing his policymaking duties, it cost him consideration for future appointments that would require Senate confirmation. Activity by stakeholders had a more direct effect on substantive institutional issues, although none leading to broad changes in overall policy or outside of the specific case in which the stakeholder was involved.

Reynolds's willingness to meet with his critics, explain his position, and openly confront opponents helped the Administration withstand challenges to its CRIPA enforcement from both Congress and stakeholders. The other direction from which pressure could be brought to bear on the Administration's policy was from within the Department of Justice itself, primarily from careerists who in effect acted as internal stakeholders.

• 6 •

Reaction from Within: Careerists

Justice Department attorneys are highly educated people operating in a verbal, contentious environment. Golden (1992) found that Justice attorneys by nature are inclined to argue more constantly and forcefully against policies with which they disagree. The fact that the careerists in the agency involved in CRIPA implementation are attorneys, coupled with the pronounced shift in scope and direction of enforcement efforts, suggest that internal opposition to the administrative strategy would be strong. This chapter examines how the attorneys in the Special Litigation Section viewed and responded to the Administration's pursuit of its CRIPA preference.

OPINION OF ENFORCEMENT

Civil rights enforcement tends to attract attorneys who are liberal and support the active role of the government in protecting civil rights. The ideology and political preference of Special Litigation survey respondents bears this out.[1] Of 26 respondents, 15 categorized themselves as "liberal" or "very liberal," while only four identified themselves as "conservative" and only one as "very conservative." Twenty-one of the 25 respondents did not vote for Ronald Reagan in either 1980 or 1984. The four who did support Reagan in at least one of the elections began working at the Department of Justice after May 1983.

The respondents' opinion of CRIPA enforcement reflects this ideology. Although the Justice Department was viewed as somewhat active in investigating institutions (20 out of 26 respondents), careerists felt the investigations lacked substance. Too much time was spent negotiating with states (10 out of 19), and the resulting consent decrees were too general (16 out of 21). The Administration's view of the constitutional rights of institutionalized persons was too narrow (22 out of 26), and the Administration was too accommodating toward states (16 out of 21). Overall, respondents believed that too few investigations were opened (15 out of 21), too few lawsuits were filed (17 out of 20), and that the scope of CRIPA enforcement was too lenient (18 out of 23). Almost unanimously, respondents reported that at some point in their employment they disagreed with Reynolds or his deputies in a CRIPA case (25 out of 26).

The survey results and written record indicate that careerists generally did not feel that the Administration's enforcement of CRIPA was adequate. How they indicated that dissatisfaction and the way that response varied over time is a more complex story.

ACTION TAKEN BY CAREERISTS

Voice

As the new Reagan Administration was going through its transition and taking shape, the attitude of careerists can best be described as wary optimism. Those attorneys who had worked under Presidents Nixon or Ford believed that the nature of civil rights enforcement would remain relatively unchanged, as they felt it had during those administrations. One attorney remembers discussing his concerns with a careerist of long tenure, who told him, "What I could expect was we would not be pushing to make new law, that private plaintiffs would be doing that, but that their experience was the law that had been established would be strongly enforced."[2] Even though Ronald Reagan had made some disparaging comments during the campaign about civil rights enforcement, the careerists did not expect that civil rights of the disabled or institutionalized would be a target of sweeping change. While a change in some aspects of civil rights enforcement was felt to be inevitable after Reynolds was nominated, especially where remedies such as busing or quotas were involved, "it was less clear that he was going to have a view one way or the other with respect to disability issues."

A Deputy Assistant Attorney General during this transition period did not share this optimism. As she put it, "Against the backdrop of the rhetoric . . . we assumed nothing was inviolate" (Interview with Lynn Walker Huntley, 1995). Such supervisory attorneys naturally had the earliest contact with the new Administration, and began with an effort to convey the scope of institutional abuses by showing new appointees a videotape of jail guards beating an inmate, as recorded by the jail's own security camera. The then-Chief of the Special Litigation Section, Robert Plotkin, described the tape as "awful" and "graphic," even for persons inured to such matters. But the reaction of Attorney General Smith and his Special Assistant, future Whitewater Independent Counsel Kenneth Starr, was not what Plotkin expected: "I remember French Smith and Starr were like, you know, what time is it, I gotta get out of here, don't bother me with this stuff. . . . It was just . . . their lack of sensitivity and response to that was, I mean, that said a lot to me about what was going on."

Plotkin related that a similar effort to educate was attempted when Reynolds was nominated to be Assistant Attorney General:

We put together a photo album of pictures of people in institutions after they had been brutalized or beaten or raped or neglected or sat in their feces for three days or whatever. Photographs that we had used in different trials as exhibits and we just put together this whole book. And we were convinced no one could look at this book without being totally moved. Brad proved us wrong when he finally came to look at it. . . . He looked at it the way, like when you go to somebody's house that you barely know and they bring out their wedding album or something. . . . "That's very nice, you have a very nice family," that kind of review of something.

The education process then moved to specific cases and issues, and line attorneys became involved in turn as their cases underwent scrutiny, usually when pleadings were sent to the front office for review. Travel schedules and the nature of when issues arose in cases for a time insulated some attorneys from direct contact with Reynolds, and initial policy directives were communicated through a sort of trial-and-error process.

Frequently in the course of what attorneys expected to be a routine review, Reynolds would raise questions about litigation stances that had previously never been at issue. Several attorneys said they were stunned to find themselves summoned to meetings where they were asked to justify positions that had always been advanced as a matter of course. "Reynolds would ask a lot of questions about things that we thought were settled, like 'Where in the Constitution does it say that people need soap?' and I would write serious memos explaining." "Brad would respond, 'I'm with you on policy, but it's not a constitutional issue.' He had a real blind spot because he didn't think that anything you could tell him would convince him that this was in the Constitution."

Arthur Peabody, who replaced Plotkin as Section Chief, questioned whether Reynolds was really interested in answers to the questions he raised, stating, "I now identify that many of the exercises were an effort to ascertain how many angels could sit on the head of a pin." Some attorneys resented the review and questions, but others thought they were legitimate, and believed that as long as Reynolds was willing to meet to discuss his concerns, there was a possibility that he could be persuaded to adopt a different point of view. Deputy Assistant

Attorney General Huntley said that although Reynolds had an inquisitive mind, it was open only so far as was necessary to gather the information he needed to apply his ideological views. After that, "His habit was not to seek the information" (Interview with Lynn Walker Huntley, 1995).

Meetings with Reynolds became "more of a big deal" after the Special Litigation Section was moved out of the main Justice building. Although Reynolds continued to agree to meet and was viewed by the attorneys as generally accessible, more attorneys began to feel that they were not getting anywhere. One described the meetings as "mixed bags. The good news was, they would let you make your case. The bad news was, they were so dense, the people were so dense, that they could not seem to understand your positions. They didn't get it." The attorney went on to say that while Reynolds was "amenable to letting us open our mouth in his presence . . . it's just that it went in his ear and it never did register. . . . I never, ever had the feeling that we were making any points on any issue with him. I mean, there was no sense of give and take or really genuinely trying to arrive at the best position. It was, he would listen and then reconfirm his position on whatever it was."

The tenor of the meetings during the first years of the Administration, especially when coupled with the emotional and even life-threatening nature of the issues involved, made the process even more frustrating for some of the attorneys. "It was a polarized time, and he was a polarizing man." Reynolds was characterized as "blunt," "less than respectful," and "not what you would call an affable fellow." His style of communicating is "very succinct, [which] comes across as brusque." He used the same manner whether he was dealing with line attorneys or the Section supervisors: "I think he included the Section Chiefs pretty much in his overall declaration of war against all career people." Certainly early on, the impression was that Reynolds did not trust the line attorneys—"it came out in every word he used." He rarely couched his opinions in language designed to soften their impact, and was overheard to state that he "wasn't going to be anyone's friend." One attorney likened an invitation to come to a meeting with Reynolds to "being summoned to the mountain just to be dressed down." The Section Chief himself was chastised, in a meeting of other Section Chiefs, when he was enthusiastically reporting that Reynolds had approved a request to intervene in an ongoing institutional case. Reynolds curtly responded, "I'm sure the Governor of [the state sued] doesn't feel that way." But except when reacting to direct emotional attacks, Reynolds's written statements on policy issues were measured in tone, and used noninflammatory language.

In a way, Reynolds's professional detachment was one of the hardest things for career attorneys to accept. The plight of institutionalized persons, witnessed first-hand by the attorneys, colored their willingness to accept Reynolds's directives. One attorney said that he "never had a case where somebody didn't die before or during the investigation," and that frequently he would cry on flights home from institutional tours. Another said, "The thing that was so frustrating was that Brad didn't seem to understand that these were human beings." One Section supervisor, trying to mediate a dispute between line attorneys and Reynolds, described how he became so upset after a meeting with Reynolds that he rushed to a restroom and became physically ill: "And it was just one of those totally nonsensical, insensitive, cruel, stupid positions that he expressed to me in his totally cold way and he just got me. I could have pounced on the man, but better than that, I vomited" (Interview with John MacCoon, 1994). Several other former Section attorneys were moved to tears during their interviews when describing their memories of and frustrations with Reynolds. During the first years of the Administration, the Section was described as "constantly" at odds with Reynolds, and the disagreements as "visceral."

At least initially, attorneys were frequently given opportunities to make their case to Reynolds or his assistants, but usually with little effect. "We kept pummeling Brad and his deputies with what we thought," but "it's fair to say that we were afforded no discretion in anything that was of any significance." Said a supervisory attorney, "I suppose it would have been better and saved everybody time and stress if he'd have just closed his door and said, 'I'm going to be the sole attorney in this Division and you guys can just sit there and look for other jobs or read what I'm putting out or read the newspaper or whatever,' cause that's about as much use as most of us were" (Interview with John MacCoon, 1994). For pleadings in which Reynolds insisted upon massive changes, he often would do the editing and rewriting himself. Occasionally a Reynolds deputy would stand over a line attorney to ensure that desired revisions were made. The distrust was mutual.

The back-and-forth efforts to persuade Reynolds essentially culminated with the issuance of the *Youngberg* memo and its aftermath. The Section quickly responded to Reynolds in a memo drafted by a senior attorney, contending that Reynolds's interpretation of the case was flawed. A rather perfunctory meeting was held between Reynolds and his deputies and Section representatives. When that meeting didn't change Reynolds's view, concerned members of the Section reconvened to discuss strategy. In a divisive move, the Section sent Reynolds another memo, this one focusing on the broad scope of remedies that could be sought even under Reynolds's narrow interpretation. Some Section attorneys felt that sending the second memo was a mistake, because by accepting Reynolds's memo as a premise, the Section was acquiescing to a limited interpretation that would then become the upper boundary for the rights that could be redressed. The *Youngberg* memo thus marked two changes in the view that careerist voice could be effective in altering policy—it caused a rift between advocates in the Section on how far they should carry a fight with Reynolds, and for many, it marked an end to their hope that Reynolds was "educable." As one said, "After *Youngberg*, fluidity ended."

In lieu of direct persuasion on the issues, a different tack was taken to try to get Reynolds to adopt a more sympathetic view of the institutionalized—taking him on a tour of a D.C. facility for the mentally retarded. For the supervisory attorney on the tour, the experience was similar to that described when Reynolds was shown the album of photographs:

His whole demeanor through the whole thing was, I got the impression, of how he was going through because he said he would and at least you couldn't say that he never went to a place. But it was having no impact, he never made any comments about how terrible it is or you poor people or anything that indicated sympathy or empathy. It was just like he was going through the motions because we had asked him to, and he didn't want it to be said by any newspaper that he wouldn't go to visit the ones in his own town. It was more of covering himself than out of any desire to learn anything or have his perceptions impacted in any way, and it certainly didn't. He was the same old Brad after that that he was before. (Interview with John MacCoon, 1994)

When it became apparent after this initial period of voice that careerists would have little success in getting Reynolds to adopt their point of view, other forms of communication and protest were tried. Some attorneys who disagreed with revised pleadings refused to sign them (6 out of 25 respondents), and 4 of 25 respondents asked to be taken off a case, usually as their last protest before exiting. These actions were seen as ways to convey to Reynolds and his staff the depth of the attorneys' beliefs and disagreement, and one attorney reported that a Deputy Attorney General expressed surprise that the issue meant so much to him. Careerists also worked through counsel for private plaintiffs in cases that had them, and would tell them when Justice could not make a particular argument so that the other attorneys could. But, with the exception of the Section Chief, none of the vocal, senior career attorneys maintained their fight very long, most of them departing within two years of Reynolds's confirmation, with all of them gone by the end of 1983. The prevailing attitude was summed up by one senior attorney who recalled, "You're spending more of your time strategizing about how to get something around your own side or how to package it. When you're negotiating with the other side it's difficult enough, but when you have to spend more time thinking about how to negotiate with your own people . . . I didn't want to use my creativity that way."

Attorneys who began work in 1983 and thereafter had a more favorable view of Reynolds's willingness to listen and be persuaded than did the attorneys who preceded them, although the later-arriving attorneys actually had less opportunity to meet directly with him. Some of these attorneys found ways to work effectively with Reynolds. The attorney most successful at persuading Reynolds to adopt broader remedies in CRIPA enforcement had a number of attributes going for her, including an appreciation of the most effective way to pique Reynolds's interest and command his attention.

Even during the early years of the Administration, Reynolds would sometimes take strong action when he had personally become involved in a case "and had become infuriated with the other side." It was as though in certain instances, his penchant for legal advocacy superseded his philosophy of nonintervention in a state's affairs. This attitude was especially pronounced in situations where a state resisted Justice efforts to gain access to facilities in order to conduct investigations, a situation that did not then involve substantive policy issues. For example, in the first lawsuit filed under CRIPA, one to compel access to an institution, Reynolds flatly told the reluctant local U.S. Attorney that the U.S. Attorney, no matter who he was, *would* sign off on the Complaint, in effect threatening him with replacement if he did not support the court action.

The attorney who was able to turn this aggressiveness to her advantage succeeded because of her own background and personality, as well as the circumstances of her hiring, being the person who cornered Reynolds in an elevator after she had tried for years to be hired. Although an advocate of rights of the institutionalized, prior to coming to Justice she had interacted closely with parents opposed to deinstitutionalizing their children, gaining experience in how to deal effectively with persons who held views different from her own. A person of single-minded determination, she was described by the Section Chief as "a very committed, knowledgeable, hard worker, who just has a very nice way with people." These characteristics, coupled with her arrival after the departure of the Section's most outspoken attorneys, made significant inroads with Reynolds.

She viewed her work as a mission, taking every possible opportunity to interact with Reynolds, such as sitting next to him on plane trips and making small talk. As she described it:

My whole goal and whole agenda were . . . to get to [Reynolds] as much as possible, as quickly as possible, and have as much of an impact. . . . I didn't feel any boundaries, I didn't feel any qualms, I didn't feel like I had to respect protocol, well, I certainly wasn't afraid of him. . . . I was just always a believer that the more involved someone was, the more invested they were. And that as long as I could invest and involve someone in the facts, then I believed that their heart would follow.

She succeeded in establishing an atmosphere of trust and professionalism that Reynolds admitted made an impression on him:

She is dedicated, the most dedicated person I've seen through this whole area . . . wonderful. But somebody who . . . had a different view of CRIPA and the institutionalized persons' agenda than I did, and who was in my view, as thoughtful and . . . she worked, she fought with me every step of the way. Sometimes she persuaded me that she was right and sometimes I persuaded her that I was right. What came out of it, I think, was a very positive sort of approach. . . . (Interview with William Bradford Reynolds, 1993)

The attorney set up meetings between Reynolds and experts in the field, prepped him and briefed him before the meetings, invited him to attend conferences, and encouraged him to participate on professional panels. In perhaps her most significant act, she invited Reynolds to go on a substantive tour of a mental retardation facility by telling him of the interest of the state's Governor and Attorney General in the investigation. She recounted a moving interaction Reynolds had with a young resident of the facility during the tour:

It seems out of nowhere [girl's name], age three, came running up to us, and I'll never forget, threw her arms around Brad's legs. And he's so big, and she was so, so, so tiny. She barely came up to his knees. And she just clung to him. And he looked down at her, and she was just the most, just the most adorable, a beautiful little girl. And he couldn't believe that she was here. She was in a ward where people were visibly much more significantly retarded than she was. And he picked her up, and I also remember that she stroked his face. . . . He was just absolutely smitten with [her]. And she was with us for the rest of the tour. And he of course wanted to know why was this little girl here. And that was the beginning of being able to get all of the kids out of [the institution], a very dramatic stance for him to take.

The description of this tour and Reynolds's appreciation of the human element are in stark contrast to the earlier tour attorneys conducted with Reynolds, and illustrate this attorney's effective use of voice. She explained her perspective of Reynolds, which contrasted with the attitude of many of the attorneys who had preceded her, saying, "I really did view and treat Brad as a human being, and just as any human being that I would interact with, whereas it would never cease to amaze me the whole time that Brad was here how other people reacted to him, and how Arthur [Section Chief Peabody] in particular had this phenomenal hands-off, almost reverence."

Her efforts continued throughout the rest of the Administration, but she said that persuading Reynolds never became easy. Her effective approach, although perhaps something that few could emulate, illustrates the positive attributes some attorneys saw in Reynolds: he could be persuaded, even if the change was incremental; he was accessible—"you may not have won the debate, but you had the debate"; "he was willing to learn material and to dive in fairly thoroughly"; and "he had the law at his fingertips." Attorneys who worked under both Reynolds and later his successor in the Bush Administration spoke nostalgically of Reynolds's accessibility (illustrated in part by universal reference to him by his first name), and of his academic interest in issues.

Subsequent to 1983, other attorneys who felt they had success in advancing their positions relied primarily on their ability to avoid politicization in making their substantive arguments. In one instance, after a conservative attorney had responded to a Reynolds question in ideological rhetoric, another attorney on the case gave Reynolds a straightforward answer, without spin. Reynolds told her that he appreciated the candor, stating, "In my position I frequently get told the things people think I want to hear, not what I need to know."

Reynolds's acknowledgement of attorneys' self-censorship comports with the experience of several line attorneys who worked in the Section after 1983. Whereas prior to that time attorneys who disagreed with Reynolds would frequently argue their position directly to him, Section leadership later began to perform more of a gatekeeping role. Fewer matters were brought directly to Reynolds, and attorneys were limited to exercising their voice at the Section level. This change came about for two reasons. First, the departure of senior, experienced attorneys made it easier to contain dissent because new attorneys lacked self-confidence in substantive matters and often were unaware of policy nuances. As one new attorney explained, "It took a while to understand the disparity between the rest of the field and where we were." Second, after the first few years of confrontation on many issues, there was a conscious decision by the Section Chief to pursue only those matters "where we thought there was a reasonable opportunity to make an inroad" (Interview with Arthur Peabody, 1994). As a result, with the exception of the attorney previously discussed at length, after 1983 attorneys generally did not argue their points outside of the Section, except in those increasingly rare cases where Section leadership agreed to involve Reynolds.

Attorneys became frustrated by their inability to argue back. One described how a pleading was returned from the front office with a big red "x" through an entire page, with no explanation for the deletion. He went to the Section Chief and asked what was wrong—was it badly written? Did it go against policy? The Section Chief said there was nothing that could be done—"that's just the way it is." Because the Section leadership would not pursue many issues, most attorneys felt they could do nothing more, and that going around the Section Chief would "undermine the chain of command." Even the previously-described attorney who had established a direct relationship with Reynolds faced efforts to discourage her from attending a second meeting she had scheduled with one of Reynolds's assistants, being told by the Deputy Section Chief, "If [the assistant] cannot exercise the good sense and management skills to better control his time, or how much time he should spend on things, then we should manage it for him and not show up at the second meeting." The early years of the Administration were characterized by a great deal of voice on the part of careerists, but to a large extent there was silence on policy issues after that. "I didn't feel like the message of the Section was going out . . . [or] that we were presenting our expertise in a good way."

Several of the attorneys who left Special Litigation within the first three years of Reynolds's arrival continued to express their disagreement after their departure. At least four attorneys wrote law review or other articles about the Civil Rights Division and testified at congressional hearings, while several others spoke to or provided documentation to reporters or congressional staffers. Of the attorneys who formally conveyed their disagreements to persons outside of Justice, none had been hired during the Reagan Administration. Attorneys hired after 1983 who disagreed with CRIPA enforcement contained their dissent within the Department.

An example of the difference in exercise of voice is given by an attorney hired in 1983, who despite personal disagreements with Reynolds, felt that she should not express those disagreements even to him because it was his prerogative to call the shots, not hers. When she made the decision to leave Justice for reasons other than policy disagreement, she asked for and was granted an exit interview with Reynolds. In describing the interview, she said:

My parting shot was that we should be more rigorous. We could thrive when we were allowed to do our work, and that to impose the political agenda on line attorneys made no sense. Those fights should happen on the Hill, they should develop policy, give policy, but not in the life of the case. Don't do it at the line level—it's destructive, it's divisive, you don't get what you want. Work it at the levels where you create policy, and then I can do my work or not because I know what the reality is.

The attorney reported that Reynolds was respectful and seemed interested. The process of leaving Special Litigation was a more adversarial process for many others, however, particularly those who had worked under previous Administrations.

Exit

There is no formal documentation of the total number of attorney departures from the Special Litigation Section during the Reagan Administration. The rate of turnover was characterized by the Section Chief as "massive" initially, and steady throughout (Interview with Arthur Peabody, 1994). At one point, departures were so frequent that a Deputy Section Chief, giving a speech at a going-away party, joked that it was the "weekly farewell party."

While admitting that this statement may have slightly exaggerated the rate, and that it was more like one departure a month, he said "It was clearly mass defection by career people, and it was a sad talent drain for the Division from which it will probably never recover. . . . It's like there was this fire that kind of wiped out the landscape and it's all growing back now, but it's not quite what it was and it will take a while before it's like what it was" (Interview with John MacCoon, 1994).

Many attorneys spoke of the low morale of the Section during the Reagan Administration, one saying that "on a scale of zero to ten, it was a one." New hires, especially those assumed to be hand-picked by the Administration, were "met with suspicion" and with the "barest of collegiality." The low morale and sometimes open hostility between careerists holding opposing views of enforcement hastened the departure of several attorneys.

Of the eighteen attorneys employed in Special Litigation as of January 1981, only three were still there in January 1984. One was Section Chief Arthur Peabody, who had been promoted to fill the vacancy left by Robert Plotkin's departure. Of the other two, one transferred out of the Division later in 1984. In slightly more than two years after Reynolds's appointment, there was almost complete turnover. Several of the slots had turned over more than once, meaning that attorneys hired to fill vacancies left very quickly themselves. Stories abound of attorneys just out of law school or with no legal experience in the field assigned as junior attorneys on some of the Section's major cases, only to become the lead attorney within a few weeks. In one instance, an attorney who came to the Section in November and was the fifth attorney in seniority on an important case was lead counsel by the following March.

The survey indicates that for nine respondents who began employment prior to the Reagan Administration, eight had left by November 1983. Of those eight, seven indicated that their primary reason for leaving was disagreement over CRIPA or another Administration policy. Through interviews and an examination of public records, at least three other attorneys who departed during this period fall into this category. In contrast, only five out of the thirteen respondents who began working after January 1981 left the Section primarily because of CRIPA or another policy disagreement. Three out of those five were actually hired during the Carter Administration, but did not begin employment until after the new Administration had taken office.

Despite Reynolds's assertion otherwise at his confirmation hearing, policy disagreement seems to have been a motivating force behind the initial "massive" turnover. From 1984 on, however, few of the departures (three out of twelve) were due to disagreement with Reynolds on CRIPA or other policies. A source of dissatisfaction frequently cited by those who left after December 1983 was Section leadership. Although the problems attorneys had with

Section-level decisions generally reflected Reynolds's management efforts, the result was that attorneys leaving after 1983 were much more likely to blame the Section Chief or a Deputy Chief for enforcement problems rather than Reynolds. An attorney who had worked under a previous administration offered his explanation for this tendency—newer attorneys had never seen the Section Chief in his prior role as policy advocate, and were "less inclined to give him the benefit of the doubt, not being able to see the context for his 'retreat.' . . . Those of us there before Brad arrived had no doubt at whose doorstep the blame for policy shifts should be laid" (Robert Dinerstein, personal communication, October 30, 1994).

Several factors influenced when attorneys, all of whom had tried to obtain change through voice, decided to leave. One of the earliest departures was the initial Section Chief, who left when he realized he wasn't going to be able to accomplish things within the system. "I was the first, and I just thought everybody else should have been resigning along with me" (Interview with Robert Plotkin, 1993). Plotkin's departure was noisy—he "very bluntly predicted bad things were going to happen and that he hoped it wouldn't but that's why he was leaving." An op-ed piece detailing his reasons for resigning, typed by a Departmental secretary in Plotkin's last days, appeared in the *New York Times* the Sunday after his departure (Plotkin, 1981).

Plotkin's exit and concerns about the future resulted in uncertainty among some attorneys. Although he was "generally, if not universally admired," his leaving was somewhat expected because he was seen as a political carryover from the Carter Administration. It was thought he might be "something of an alarmist," and most attorneys "were not then convinced that his warnings were accurate."

Plotkin's successor described how the exit process developed. "A lot of the original people tried to stay, and then left when the impact of the policies was felt on the cases and projects that they were personally dealing with. When it affected them personally in their work, they decided to do something" (Interview with Arthur Peabody, 1994). For some, the "something" was voice, then exit; for others, it was voice, sabotage, then exit. Said a senior attorney who tried to work within Reynolds's guidelines:

Everybody has their own threshold of frustration and tolerance. Some of the more volatile people like Plotkin left immediately because they didn't even want to see any of it. . . . It seems like some people, it was a matter of they were entrenched in their favorite cause or case and when something dire happened to it, they were out of there. . . . For others, it was just like myself, a cumulative kind of thing where at some point you reach the realization that this is not worth it, it's not going to change, and . . . you're not even having a positive effect, you're just here as a tool of the dismantling of the Civil

Rights Division, and unless you want to continue to do that, get out. (Interview with John MacCoon, 1994)

Reynolds' initial willingness to meet with attorneys and listen to their arguments led attorneys to believe that they could persuade him to change his stance. When they were unsuccessful, many left angrily. One said that despite his efforts to work within the system, he left "when I realized I had been conned. Their real goal was just to keep the bureaucrats busy writing memos within the Department, and never to enforce anything." Another told a reporter, "I resigned in great disgust. My general experience under Reynolds was that things just wouldn't move. It seemed almost like he was attempting to make us believe that things would start to move if we would just write the memorandum differently, and no matter how we wrote it we'd just keep getting the memo back" (Taylor, 1984 [June 22], quoting Adjoa Aieyotoro).

Leaving was a hard decision. For many, coming to the Civil Rights Division had been the fulfillment of a life-long dream. Some worried that by leaving, they were helping to further weaken the Division: "Maybe if I had stayed, there would at least have been one more person doing some good." Others were concerned about how their continued presence would be viewed by stakeholders they cared about. "Had I stayed I would have been trotted out as the apologist to women and minorities for efforts to undo the rights I had worked so hard to achieve" (Interview with Lynn Walker Huntley, 1995).

Not all departures were voluntary. One attorney was given 30 days to resign; one was facing a 30-day suspension without pay and involuntary transfer out of the Section; one was removed from his primary case and given no new assignments; and Timothy Cook, according to Reynolds, was on the verge of being fired when he "jumped the gun" and resigned (Interview with William Bradford Reynolds, 1993). It was Cook who exited with the biggest splash, sending the *New York Times* and the *Washington Post* his 33-page resignation memo with its 179 pages of attachments (primarily internal communications) (Cook, 1983 [October 18]). Cook's action precipitated an investigative report by a Washington television station, and undoubtedly provided the incentive for the House and Senate hearings conducted in the fall of 1983. After that resignation, attorneys rarely requested exit interviews and no departing attorney left with much fanfare or attempt to convey general disagreement outside of the Department. Most of the old guard had already left, and Cook's efforts were legendary in their scope. The few remaining attorneys with serious policy disagreements had little energy left to wage a fight, and the belief that it would not do much good anyway. The activities of the Administration had been conveyed exhaustively to the media, Congress, and stakeholders, with little change in the level of CRIPA enforcement.

Reynolds testified in his confirmation hearing that because departing attorneys had other jobs, he did not view them as having resigned in protest. The interviews revealed that all but one of the attorneys did move directly into new positions, and at that time there were many employment opportunities for experienced Justice attorneys. But in several instances attorneys had to settle for less-than-desirable positions after a hurried search. Of the persons who departed because of policy disagreements, only a handful went directly into a job that they thought was a step up from their Justice position, or at least how they had viewed it under the previous Administration. One attorney, who had taken a five-month leave of absence from Special Litigation because of a disagreement with policy, finally resigned without a job to go to and remained unemployed for six months.

Some of the more junior attorneys who left in the first two years of the Administration did so because of an indirect effect of administrative policies—the departure of their mentors. Several mentioned how they had been attracted to the Department because of the opportunity to work with attorneys of great stature who had litigated landmark cases in the field, attorneys who had "talent comparable with the best law firms." The remaining attorneys were deprived of expertise, institutional memory, continuity in long-term cases, and even faced a lack of credibility when they would try to take over negotiations with state defendants. A supervisory attorney said that the loss of attorneys who were experienced in institutional litigation meant a loss of the "common knowledge of seasoning and strategy," of "experience that has been leavened." Newer attorneys, especially those assigned to ongoing cases, would make mistakes others would not, and their presence would "embolden adversaries to try tricks that they knew a seasoned person would avoid" (Interview with Lynn Walker Huntley, 1995).

The initial months after Reynolds began were characterized by a camaraderie among attorneys trying to fight a common enemy, only to be followed by demoralization as attorneys watched their colleagues leave, some under duress. Describing how she saw a "noose being put around the neck of attorneys of long stature," one young attorney said, "If they could treat someone who had been there for ten years like that, imagine how they could treat someone who had been there for less than two years." The rate of departure of experienced attorneys did not concern Reynolds:

I never thought that if we needed to find people we'd have a hard time finding them. I never thought that it'd be hard to replace. . . . I don't believe that I need to have an expert in institutionalized persons law to fill a gap that is left or vacancies left by somebody who has become an expert. . . . And if you know how to litigate—if you are a good lawyer—then you can learn that area. . . . I was never concerned that I would be left on a ship without a bunch of sailors. (Interview with William Bradford Reynolds, 1993)

There was a decline over time in the size of the pool of applicants from which to hire replacements, however, in one year dropping to 217 applicants for jobs in the entire Civil Rights Division, down from a normal range of between 1500 and 1800 (Interview with Arthur Peabody, 1994). The Section Chief and one of the Deputy Section Chiefs also noted a decrease in the caliber of attorneys interested in being hired. Hiring decisions emphasized "balance," with the Administration's goal being to hire persons who were less "personally wrought up" in the policy issues and could "tone down" the situation.

The relationship between the Section and Reynolds seemed to improve with the passage of time, in part "because the real outspoken people left." The departure of some attorneys was viewed with relief by their recently-hired colleagues: "I just found his constant grousing, bad-mouthing Reynolds and his administration was not conducive to doing our job right." From the perspective of the old-timers who tried to remain, however, the newly-hired attorneys sometimes added to their frustrations. A person who was seen to be a "political hire" was referred to as a "true believer," and a new hire who didn't make waves was criticized because she "never raised her head, she tried to do things at the margins."

Some of the experienced attorneys who left the Section in the first few years were so frustrated and angry about enforcement that before their departure they took action that was meant to impede the efforts of the Administration in achieving its policy preference. These are the careerists who can be said to have adopted a strategy of sabotage.

The Saboteurs

To a certain extent, whether an act constitutes sabotage is in the eyes of the beholder. Some of the acts discussed in this section were not viewed as sabotage by the actors, but rather were seen as an appropriate response to the Administration's failure to enforce a duly enacted law. One attorney explained that he felt his drastic acts were justified because he owed a duty to Congress and the American people to see that legislation was enforced. For the purpose of categorizing acts under this heading, sabotage is defined as acts that are intended to subvert the Administration's pursuit of its policy preference.

The mildest acts falling within this definition were those taken in cases where there were plaintiff parties in addition to or other than Justice, meaning those cases in which Justice was an intervenor or *amicus*. Under the policy direction of the Reagan Administration, Justice attorneys frequently found themselves at odds with parties with whom they had historically been aligned, and in some instances were asked to take positions in opposition to those that they themselves had previously advanced. Every attorney interviewed who had worked on such cases prior to Reynolds coming in, as well as several newly-hired attorneys, found ways to assist the other parties in advancing positions Justice no longer would.

The specific actions taken varied, including: telling other attorneys that Justice would not be seeking certain remedies, but offering reports, Justice-provided experts, or other means to help the parties obtain the remedies themselves; indicating to the judge or someone else who would tell the judge that the Justice attorneys did not personally share the views they were formally advancing; going beyond minimal direct or cross examination so as to elicit testimony favorable to another party; and choosing not to file discretionary pleadings such as briefs where it was believed that a brief that could pass review would hurt the other parties' case. In taking such action, attorneys "managed to get some things said that had Brad been looking over our shoulder every second, we would not have gotten done." One attorney explained that he did not see this as "outright disobeying." The attorneys, he said, could return and say, "I'm sorry, Brad, the judge did it, we didn't do it." Similarly, after furnishing private attorneys with information or advice enabling them to get an expansive ruling, Section attorneys would report the outcome to Reynolds and blame the outside attorneys.

In at least two instances, acts of this sort resulted in disciplinary action against attorneys and ultimately led to their departure. In one case, an attorney admittedly "under very strict orders not to make any proposal that differed from the official party line" attempted to present a conciliatory position to the court that he felt would have settled a dispute between the private plaintiffs and the State. In making his argument in court, he tried to follow his orders by asserting that he was "taking off his DOJ hat" before offering the conciliatory proposal. Someone present in court, most likely the State defendants, communicated the gist of his argument to Reynolds, who demanded to see a transcript. The attorney resigned in the face of 30 days of leave without pay and an involuntary transfer to another Section.

In a more flagrant breach of direction, another attorney filed three consent decrees that had not been reviewed or approved even within the Section. Again, the State defendants in the case notified Reynolds, and the attorney was given 30 days to resign (Interview with Arthur Peabody, 1994). In a statement about his departure, the attorney said, "I represented the classic example of a good lawyer gone sour" (Confirmation of William Bradford Reynolds, 1985, p. 945). Observing the kamikaze actions of such attorneys was uplifting for some of the others, one of whom said, "We all kind of applauded, but we said 'better you than me,' because I can't afford to lose my job."

Outside of actions in court, several attorneys leaked documents to Congress or the media in efforts to bring pressure on the Administration. One reporter in particular was thought to have talked to almost every attorney then in the Section. Not all of these leaks and contacts resulted in media attention, but the efforts of two attorneys are particularly noteworthy. One was provoked to act when an important pleading, to which he had devoted several months of hard work, was summarily rejected in concert with his removal from the case. The attorney had generally described the nature of the pleading with Reynolds while drafting it, and had strived to keep it within the guidelines of which he was aware, maintaining close contact with the Section Chief about the scope of the pleading and his progress. The rejection caught him totally by surprise. After learning what happened, he then took every step he could think of to draw attention to the situation—letting everyone who could do anything (including talk to the media) know the details, calling congressional staffers and giving them copies of documents, and contacting a stakeholder group in the state where the target institution was located and giving them enough information to permit them to enter the litigation to thwart the Department's position. Up until this happened, he had been a loyal attorney who thought he was unaffected by what had happened to others. In describing why he was provoked to act, he said, "I thought it was wrong, and I was just not willing to sit back and allow it to happen. I would say I was fighting, really, without thinking about my future." From that point on, he was planning to leave the Section. He believes, as does another attorney with personal knowledge, that a desirable job offer he received from another Division in Justice was retracted because of Reynolds's intervention.

Section attorney Timothy Cook fought the longest and hardest of any careerist, on issues involving several of the Section's cases as well as overall civil rights enforcement. Now deceased, Cook left behind an array of testimony and writings outlining his disagreements. Many of the attorneys interviewed mentioned Cook as the suspected perpetrator of some of the more notorious leaks during the contentious years, such as the leak of Reynolds's *Youngberg* memo to the press and stakeholders. One attorney remembers going with several attorneys to meet with a reporter over dinner, a meeting arranged by Cook, at which the topic of discussion was how to strategize the upcoming media blitz. Cook would frequently talk to reporters by telephone in his office, and once called another attorney to come to Cook's office to talk to a reporter who was then present. The attorney recalls that he blurted out, "You gotta be out of your mind!" As one of his colleagues put it, "Tim was a perfect example of people who, in a different context, are absolutely the people you'd want. Hardworking, creative, smart, zealous, but without that last little dollop of judgment sometimes."

Attorneys thought Cook was "effective in getting the story out" and that his actions "precluded further damage." Indeed, his tumultuous and widely-reported departure made him the only person later recalled by Reynolds as having departed the Special Litigation Section in protest. The impact he had on Reynolds was such that one attorney remembered seeing Cook's picture posted at the building security desk to ensure that he could not sneak in. The scope and nature of Cook's activities made it easier for others to remain quiet, for he was doing as thorough a job of drawing attention as anyone could. Even within the Section, though, there was concern about his actions. "He lost some effectiveness, people didn't trust him, he wasn't subtle." Another summed Cook up by saying, "Tim always did everything with a flair. He enjoyed that. He enjoyed 'stabbing at the forces of evil.' "

One other type of behavior falls within this category—acts that went against the interest of colleagues, even those sympathetic to the actor's viewpoint. Although uncommon, some instances were related where, in an effort to undermine the Administration, colleagues were "set up." An attorney who frequently agreed with Reynolds felt that he was the target of sabotage by attorneys with whom he worked. Also within this category is an instance where it was alleged a Section supervisor, purportedly to create a confrontation, failed to communicate to a line attorney that the front office had decided against making a particular argument. Another example involves an anecdote about Reynolds's alleged inactivity in a North Carolina prison case that was repeated and ultimately included in a published report critical of the Administration, despite the fact that the lead attorney, not a Reynolds fan, recalls that Reynolds had pursued the matter aggressively. Last, an attorney who was asked to sign a letter to Congress declined to do so, and later found out that his name had been put on the document without his permission. These admittedly isolated instances illustrate that the saboteurs viewed the ends as justifying the means, even when their own colleagues could be harmed.

Despite pervasive policy disagreement among holdover careerists, few resorted to sabotage. Several mentioned they felt there were professional and ethical constraints on communicating internal matters outside of the Department, especially while they were still employed. Additionally, as one noted, the nature of the policy disagreement did not lend itself to "capsulization on the evening news." Most carryover attorneys initially tried to stay and work within the system after the new Administration took office.

Loyalty

Despite a commitment to traditional civil rights enforcement and their disagreement with the CRIPA policy preference, several holdovers from prior administrations initially felt they could live with the new constraints and still do productive work. Reynolds seemed intellectually interested in the issues, and he was viewed as having a legitimate right to raise some questions. "Although I disagreed with his policies, Reynolds was approved by the Senate and I was not. . . . I disliked their policies on a lot of things, but I thought, I'm a lawyer, not a politician. I also felt that he had a right to ask these questions—so what if I think it's ridiculous?"

Such attorneys took Reynolds's statements at face value, and tried to do what they believed he wanted. Attorneys who stayed despite disagreement were motivated by the hope that they could effect change from within. One explained why he tried to stay:

Once a decision was made, I did not as some people did, just feel like I could defy them. . . . I would carry [Reynolds's directive] out so far as that I never carried out anything that I thought was unethical in the strictest sense or illegal, but certainly I was not proud of having to participate in implementing his decisions. [We stayed as long as we did] because we thought maybe reason or compromise would prevail and that we would at least make some dent in his policies.

Other than the Section Chief, the few career attorneys who remained for more than two or three years into the Administration did not appear to harbor major policy differences with the Administration. When they ultimately left, it was for more traditional reasons, such as new career opportunities.

The Section Chief, despite his own differences with Reynolds, supported him to the extent of drafting background materials for his use in responding to criticism at oversight hearings, even though Reynolds had not asked him to do so (Interview with Arthur Peabody, 1994). Peabody explained that, "If you stayed, and you were doing legitimate professional work . . . there is some element of investment here that whatever the response is or whatever the attack is, the response should include some objective information about what was done."

Their expectation of what the enforcement level would be influenced whether careerists were loyal to the Administration's policy preference, forming an alliance with the new attorneys. It was very difficult for careerists who had known a different approach to and level of enforcement to buy into a lesser scheme. An attorney who arrived in 1983 described this as the difference in the "contract" attorneys came in with. He felt that careerists from the prior administrations believed:

You're here to push the envelope on this law, let's take this law and run with it. We're the guys who made the law, let's take it and go. My impression was a lot of guys came in with that contract and they were being true to that contract, but that wasn't a contract that really should have been given. . . . I felt that it was a shame that they didn't operate within the limitations that the new Administration had the right to impose.

One of the old careerists who departed fairly quickly agreed, saying that in retrospect he could appreciate the legitimacy of Reynolds's approach and that under similar circumstances now, he would try to stay longer and work within the constraints.

From 1984 on, the attorneys who can be considered loyal can be categorized by their motivation: those who strongly disagreed with the Administration's policy preferences, but felt that it was important to work for change within the system (*dissenting loyalists*); those who agreed with the Administration (*assenting loyalists*); and those who didn't spend much time thinking about whether they agreed or disagreed—they were there to do a job (*apoliticals*). Two dissenting loyalists, strong advocates for the rights of persons with disabilities, explained why they came to work in 1983 even though they were aware of problems within the Section, including Timothy Cook's widely-publicized resignation: "I had a very strong belief on my part that I could change from within and that it was an important role to play. . . . One thing that I always wanted to do, was to be in a situation where, . . . although I adhered to certain beliefs, to be able to try and convince people who disagreed with me and who had the power to make decisions that other decisions should be made." The other reflected similar feelings: "I think anybody has a responsibility, if you are a professional, to try to bring about change to the extent you can. This was my philosophy . . . you're in the system, you follow the system. You do whatever you can within the system to try to change it, try to do whatever reform you can, but if you can't, you don't use subversives."

These individuals illustrate that persons who openly disagreed with Reynolds still managed to be hired. Not all of the replacements were "Republican political operatives," as was claimed by one attorney, but they did differ from many of the departed careerists in that they accepted the constraints and would work for change through traditional internal means.

On the other hand, the assenting loyalists remained because they agreed with Reynolds. A few of these people were hired because of political connections, others just had a more conservative approach to litigation. One said that when he began, he believed "there are limits; DOJ is not the panacea." Some shared Reynolds's view of CRIPA: "There was this sort of friction between . . . some of the old-timers who felt that this Civil Rights of Institutionalized Persons Act was much more of a go-kick-butt act than to me on its face it was." "I saw the dangers of enforcing CRIPA, not just the advantages," and "I never found any barriers to taking the steps that were necessary."

Such attorneys echoed Reynolds's derision of earlier administrations who were too zealous. One said, "You had to use a little common sense, you had to look back and say, is this place really unconstitutional, or is it just a place that I would rather not spend a weekend?" These are the respondents who generally felt that the scope of enforcement was "about right," and that "we hit [the institutions] we should be hitting." One attorney in this group displayed a letter he received from Reynolds upon the attorney's departure from the Section, thanking him for "avoiding unnecessary confrontation and legal proceedings."

The final group of loyalists, the apoliticals, believed that they were hired to do a job and ruminating about political motives detracted from their mission. These attorneys did not attend or follow oversight or confirmation hearings, and are somewhat vague when asked about Section activities outside of those in which they were directly involved. Whatever Reynolds did or did not do was seen to be his prerogative as the duly appointed officer of the executive branch, and political intrigue was irrelevant. These attorneys were not apathetic about their work—they actively pursued enforcement. They were just unconcerned with motives:

I am a lawyer and my job in the Justice Department is to be a lawyer, not a politician. . . . The political guys could have their pissing matches, but the line guys had their job to do. . . . I can't be bothered with [their] little shenanigans, [their] cloak-and-dagger. . . . My job isn't to make Brad Reynolds a kinder, gentler human being . . . nor is it my job to tell Art how I think he should run Special Lit. My job is to be a soldier.

Determining what behavior constitutes loyalty and its motivation is a complex and subjective process (Withey & Cooper, 1989). The ease by which the loyalists in Special Litigation can be divided into three types helps to make this process somewhat more understandable, as well as illustrating the evolution of a moderate alliance of loyalists within the agency.

Neglect

The final type of behavior to be examined, neglect, reflects elements of both loyalty and exit. Neglect is related to loyalty because it also involves cooperative behavior (Lowery & Rusbelt, 1986). It differs from loyalty, however, in that it is cooperative through omission, not commission. Whether they agreed or disagreed with administrative policy, those falling within this category did little about it.

Golden's definition of neglect, "apathy and lethargy through careerist silence and possibly even through careerists putting less effort and enthusiasm into their work" (1992, p. 34, relying on Withey and Cooper [1989]), is used to categorize careerist behavior. Neglect may be a transition between loyalty and exit, or it may be exit without departure (Withey & Cooper, 1989). In this respect, it resembles the mildest form of sabotage—refraining from action. "The easiest way not to get the Justice Department to do something bad was to get them not to do anything at all. . . . When motions were coming up that we didn't think we could get the Department to do the right thing on, we just didn't prepare a recommendation."

The example falling within the definition of neglect most frequently cited by interviewees was that of the line attorney turned Section Chief, Arthur Peabody, who worked throughout the Reagan Administration. Attorneys spoke of how he was a "timid," "muted" individual who "didn't meet issues head on" and "conceded the debate." For example, he was said by one attorney to shun staff meetings where issues of concern could be raised, "I think the concern was, as soon as you get two or more people together, it was going to be this conspiracy. Arthur was very unwilling to deal with that, to deal with problems, to deal with issues, to deal with controversy."

Being kept in an acting capacity, Peabody said, did not have a chilling effect on his willingness to confront Reynolds, but the perception of Section attorneys is that it kept him in his place, even after his appointment was made permanent. "I think he gave out signals both upward and downward that he was going to play ball with them and, although he didn't agree, he was going to pretty much swallow that and do whatever they wanted to maintain his position." Another said, "Art was chosen because he would go along. . . . He talked a good game but that was about it." "Art didn't push, Arthur nudged, because Arthur knew that his head was on the block. Let's face it, his head would be gone." "He didn't want to leave a trail that would be followed."

Over time, there were fewer occasions when Peabody felt that issues were still open for discussion or that anything would be gained by revisiting them. The Section became more separated from the front office, and this was exacerbated by the departure of experienced, senior attorneys who were confident and assertive about pushing issues. Attorneys who came to Special Litigation after 1983 frequently cited Section management as a large source of frustration for them, in contrast to earlier attorneys who blamed Reynolds for Section inactivity. In language that illustrates how neglect can resemble exit, attorneys said Peabody "checked out," "bailed out," or was a "non-player." "Arthur was as big a roadblock as Brad and Chuck because he was afraid of pissing them off. In the privacy of his office he would say one thing, then would let them browbeat him in a meeting. . . . I knew where his heart was, but his stomach wasn't up to it." When attorneys tried to press him to go forward, they reported that he would commiserate but not take action.

Peabody disagrees that he was unresponsive to pressure from line attorneys to fight for their positions, but that he saw no point in waging hopeless battles. Although he had formerly been active in the community of those interested in institutional rights, he said he stopped going to professional conferences because when he was there he became the "point person for attack" and "it just wasn't personally comfortable" (Interview with Arthur Peabody, 1994). Ironically, he became the point person for attack from his own colleagues.

The perception that the Section Chief was not much help to them had a two-fold effect on the careerists: It kept attorneys from trying to expand the scope of their work, and it demoralized some of the otherwise loyal attorneys. One told how the minimal-form consent decrees arose: "The reason it came about was fear in this office of Brad, and feeling, ok, if we just have our fill-in-the-blanks, then we don't have to worry about what he's going to say. And the words themselves became meaningless. . . . Everything was blamed on the front office, everything was attributed to it, and I knew that that wasn't the case."

Peabody's approach kept attorneys from arguing back to Reynolds, and the self-censorship was resented: "As a matter of management . . . I think there's a question of how you present yourself to your own troops, and not presenting a kind of attitude of 'what's the use.' " One of the line attorneys, an assenting loyalist, contended that his problem with the Section Chief's inactivity was that it didn't serve Reynolds well. This attorney, in words reminiscent of Heclo's "loyalty that argues back," felt that the Section had a responsibility to provide information and argument, and to argue things hard:

There's a simple piece of advice on this one—if you're going to give up, get out. . . . As it says in *Revelations*, "If you are lukewarm, I will spit you out." I'd rather have somebody that I can honestly confront, and I can learn from that, than a guy who is just going to duck. And I can feel bad for the guy, and I do feel bad, I think it was hard for him. But I think in terms of the work and the responsibility to be a public servant, it was bad for him, it was bad for the Section, and it was demoralizing for people to work there.

Where limited enforcement of a statute is the goal of an Administration, it may seem surprising that a supporter of that goal views careerist neglect and apathy as inimical to it. The observation above, by one of the few survey respondents who indicated that he voted for Reagan, illustrates the danger of an administrative strategy that succeeds too completely—it forecloses whatever neutral competence career attorneys can exercise to the benefit of the Administration.

The withdrawal of direction by the Section Chief and the inability of careerists to have input outside the Section were viewed by careerists to affect adversely the Section's ability to pursue even limited enforcement of CRIPA. The work of the Section was described by one attorney as "completely ad hoc." Another attorney contended that new hires came in with no relevant experience and had no one to train them, did not know what was constitutionally required in institutions, and lacked the knowledge and experience to direct experts and interpret their reports. Where careerists felt that they had expertise that could assist in the better use of investigational resources, they believed the Section Chief did not care and Reynolds was uninterested: "They didn't want anything to happen anyway, it didn't really matter what resources were being wasted." The lack of any outlet to affect policy was the final straw for many loyalists, one of whom gave his advice for future administrations: "You make people feel like you may not agree with them, but at least you value their contributions."

CONCLUSION

Careerists in Special Litigation almost universal᠁ supported more rigorous enforcement of CRIPA than the Administration wi฿hed to pursue. When the Administration first took office, supervisory careerists attempted to influence policy direction through exposure of appointees to issues and the policies previously undertaken. When these efforts were unsuccessful, the holdover supervisors left. Lower-level careerists then began their own efforts to persuade, generally as issues came up in specific cases. They were met with little or no change in policy, and most left relatively quickly. Due to the emotional nature of the issues involved and the depth of belief in the correctness of their perspective, some engaged in leaks to Congress and reporters, disobeyed the approved boundaries for courtroom argument, and performed other acts of sabotage. Where the identities of the perpetrators of these acts became known, Reynolds swiftly took action against them.

After an initial two- to three-year period of great debate and massive turnover, the Section reached something of a policy equilibrium, with most disputes being confined within the Section. Because of the Section Chief's unwillingness to confront and the appointment of a Deputy who acted in a gatekeeping role, Section leadership kept many disagreements from coming to Reynolds's attention. The lack of an outlet to express policy disagreement or any mechanism for questioning decisions frustrated many careerists, most of whom did not think it appropriate to bypass the chain of command or go outside the Department. For the latter years of the Administration, Reynolds was essentially shielded from the opposing views of most Section attorneys, including those views that could have assisted the Administration in using its resources more effectively.

Although the Reagan Administration's policy preference toward CRIPA was realized, the response of careerists indicates that there may be a cost incurred by an administration bent on policy redirection through the use of a personnel-based, ideological approach. That cost encompasses adverse effects on the attainment of the policy preference itself, on administrative capacity, and even on democratic values, the putative justification for the use of an administrative strategy.

NOTES

1. The survey and results are contained in Appendix B.

2. Unless otherwise noted, quotations in this chapter are from interviews conducted with attorneys who worked in the Special Litigation Section during the Reagan Administration.

• 7 •

Administrative Implementation of CRIPA

In large part, the Reagan Administration achieved its policy preference toward CRIPA—few cases were litigated, and the remedies imposed were narrow. States were given the time and opportunity to correct their own problems, and the enforcement discretion and input of careerists was minimized. An administrative strategy can be implemented successfully by a skillful political appointee under certain circumstances.

STATUTORY CHARACTERISTICS

By the time the bill that was to become CRIPA was introduced, the high-water mark of civil rights legislation had passed. Rather than focusing solely on the wrongs to be redressed by the proposed legislation, congressional debate also included testimonials about federal government abuses of enforcement power. A post-Watergate, anti-Washington tendency, foreshadowing Ronald Reagan's 1980 election, was apparent in concerns raised during the CRIPA debate regarding how the federal government would exercise a new grant of statutory authority. The legislation dealing with the rights of a group such as institutionalized persons was especially susceptible to limitations being imposed on the enforcement of those rights, due to the lack of a vocal, sympathetic, or powerful constituency.

In order to secure passage of CRIPA, its backers had to do two things that later facilitated the Reagan Administration's limited enforcement of the law. First, the statute contained a number of procedural steps and time periods, including a waiting period of 49 days between the notice of deficiencies and filing suit, requiring a listing of the facts upon which a conclusion of deficiency was based, stating the minimal corrective measures required and proposing remedies, discussing the estimated cost of remedies and assistance available, and requiring the personal certification of the Attorney General. These provisions were included in the statute to curb the ability of the federal government to move preemptively against states, thus checking administrative zeal as well as maximizing the period during which states could take their own corrective measures. They had the additional effect of formally mandating political appointee review of bureaucratic decisions, facilitating executive control over a bureaucracy potentially too eager to file suit.

The second feature of CRIPA that facilitated an interpretation leading to limited enforcement was the vague description of the ills it was designed to cure and how that cure could be achieved. The definitions of both the conditions CRIPA was meant to redress ("egregious or flagrant conditions which deprive such persons of any rights, privileges or immunities secured or protected by the constitution or laws of the United States") and the remedies that could be sought ("the equitable relief necessary to ensure minimum corrective measures") were nonspecific and thus could be interpreted subjectively.

As Hill & Brazier (1991) note, "Compromise achieved through avoidance and ambiguity forces an administrative agency to make decisions that almost invariably will alienate some of the groups represented by the enacting coalition" (p. 384), and this is indeed what happened with CRIPA enforcement, with the statute's initial backers being the group that was alienated. The Reagan Justice Department was especially effective in pursuing its policy of limited enforcement of CRIPA because of its broad attack on the civil rights establishment, which created widescale challenges for civil rights advocates in a time of reduced ability to mount a strong opposition. The Administration's strategy of interpreting vague legislation in the manner most favorable to it was acknowledged by Attorney General William French Smith, who said that while the government must fully enforce all laws "when their validity and meaning are clear, . . . in the case of ambiguous laws, the executive branch can in good faith urge and pursue those interpretations that seem the most consistent with the intentions of Congress, the policies of the Administration, and the other laws of the land" (1991, p. 62). The fact that CRIPA was enacted late in the Carter Administration also aided the administrative strategy, for it meant there was less opportunity for a prior administration to establish an enforcement record against which comparisons could later be drawn.

ADMINISTRATIVE ACTION

One of the most striking characteristics of the Reagan Administration was its ideological clarity and consistency, and civil rights policy provides a good example (Shull, 1993). An Assistant Attorney General was selected who did not mind changing traditional civil rights enforcement, reflecting a common decision by the Administration to appoint agency heads without substantive experience. "This is seen as a strength, rather than a weakness, since they will be less likely to have strong ties to the existing interests in the area" (Ban & Ingraham, 1990, p. 110). Additionally, Reynolds attributed his freedom to speak out on issues to the knowledge that he had administrative support for positions he took:

Reagan would never have said, well, I read what Reynolds said, and I don't agree with it and he's gotta go. He wouldn't have said it, one, I made damn sure before I ever got out there, what his agenda was, so I wasn't that vulnerable. And two, he didn't waffle. He never waffled. Ronald Reagan, from the beginning to the end, set down a bunch of markers, not only in my area, but in every area, and he hung by them through thick and thin. And if you have a leader like that, and the team that he puts together understands those principles, you're gonna have a consistent administration. (Interview with William Bradford Reynolds, 1993)

Once in place, Reynolds took steps to minimize careerist discretion with unusual and intensive review of even routine matters, imposed through a requirement that all pleadings be sent to his office before being filed. Through reorganization, an additional political appointee slot was created in order to increase management capability. Reynolds prohibited attorneys from discussing cases with representatives of the media, appointing a Departmental spokesperson instead, in effect sealing off career employees (Aberbach & Rockman, 1990). Specific to Special Litigation, he required consultation with the more conservative Bureau of Prisons prior to initiating prison litigation. He made extensive changes in pleadings and met personally with state defendants in the absence of line attorneys, in both instances effectively removing line attorneys from continued influence in cases. He did not hesitate to confront attorneys and outsiders who disagreed with him, giving them a forum in which to air their opposing views. Nonetheless, he stood fast in the face of their arguments, shifting his position only incrementally, if at all. Providing an outlet, however limited, for opposing views reduced the likelihood and effectiveness of involvement by outside parties. Without an outright refusal by the Administration to meet with opponents and consider their views, critics had less on which to base their opposition, as well as less chance that a simple difference of opinion would be considered newsworthy.

In justifying Administration policy, Reynolds relied upon CRIPA legislative history and Supreme Court pronouncements in cases such as *Youngberg*, which he interpreted quickly before alternative views could be formulated so as to better control the terms of any debate. This permitted him to deflect criticism away from himself. For example, Reynolds defended his *Youngberg* memo by stating, "I simply explained that the Supreme Court had rendered a decision that had an impact on our enforcement responsibility and that we should be attentive to the Supreme Court" (Thornton, 1982, p. A2). Reliance on Supreme Court decisions made it easier for the Administration to counter criticism by characterizing disagreement as merely a difference in philosophy, rather than even debating the possibility of an erroneous interpretation on the Administration's part. In general, however, Reynolds shunned policy pronouncements such as the *Youngberg* memo, avoiding the articulation of a specific policy. Where opponents cannot rally around a clearly identified statement, it is difficult for them to mount a unified attack (Golden, 1992).

In his confirmation hearing, Reynolds responded to criticism that he unacceptably altered the Justice Department's enforcement role by interpreting the law to his liking, by observing, "Everybody who sat in this chair before me interpreted the law. . . . Nobody could sit in this chair and be about the business on a daily basis of looking at the law and trying to make the determination of whether the law fits the facts of a situation" (Williams, 1985, p. A5). This response illustrates Reynolds's ability to frame discussions by contending that he merely was doing what his predecessors had done, just with a different policy preference, and it was the different preference, not the fact of interpretation, that angered his critics.

To minimize conflict within Special Litigation, Reynolds kept the new appointees to the positions of Section Chief and Deputy Section Chief in acting capacities for lengthy periods, presumably constraining their activities to a certain extent and clearly conveying the message that he was not fully convinced of their loyalty nor satisfied with their performance. Reynolds's personal style, abrupt to the point of brusqueness, and the difficulty in getting him to change his mind, over time chilled the willingness of the Section Chief to subject himself to interactions, causing his withdrawal from issues likely to be controversial. Many new attorneys were selected for policy or political ambivalence, and generally lacked the experience or background to effectively mount substantive arguments. Further, in spite of limited enforcement, attorneys were kept busy, with no additional attorney slots approved until late in the Administration, despite the increase in enforcement authority that came with CRIPA. Attorney inactivity would have been a clear indication of enforcement inactivity, but that was not the case.

There was also a deliberate strategy regarding how to present Administration efforts to Congress, the media, and the public. Confronting critics and having some basis for the questioned action, a strategy of "candor" (Kristol, 1985, p. 64), was viewed as a way to tame the press and third parties. Also used was the technique, described in another context by Menzel (1983), of "cloak[ing] the effort or redirecting the implementation of a law in action and language that suggests strong support of statutory goals" (p. 419). Reagan himself was a master of this: "One charge I will have to admit strikes at my heart everytime I hear it: That's the suggestion that we Republicans are taking a less active approach to protecting the civil rights of all Americans. No matter how you slice it, that's just plain baloney" (Stanfield, 1983, p. 1118).

Reynolds defended enforcement efforts by stating that extended efforts to negotiate prior to litigation reflected congressional intent toward CRIPA enforcement. The statutory language emphasizing conciliation provided a basis for Reynolds's assertion, even though rarely or never litigating clearly went against congressional intent (*Civil Rights of the Institutionalized*, 1979, p. 23, colloquy between Senator Alan Simpson and Assistant Attorney General Drew Days, III). Carrying out the will of the people was also a common justification for policy stances. William French Smith, addressing objections by senior career civil rights attorneys to a shift in discrimination enforcement policy contained in a speech he had given, said, "That shift, however, was not by me but by the voters in the election of the previous November" (Smith, 1991, p. 100).

To counter criticism by stakeholders and departed attorneys that there had been a decrease in enforcement, Reynolds said, "Enforcement has been no less vigorous than in the prior Administration" (Wines, 1982, March 27, p. 537). To support this claim, Reynolds submitted to congressional committees and other critics figures for litigation across the entire Division, which did appear somewhat comparable to prior efforts. By not breaking the figures down section by section, however, Reynolds was able to create the impression of activity across the Division, whereas in fact a breakdown showed that the overall statistics were due primarily to activity in the Criminal Section of the Civil Rights Division, which remained active during the Reagan Administration (Washington Council of Lawyers, 1983). The continued and even increased activity of the Criminal Section made it possible for Smith to truthfully say that "the budget and number of employees in the Civil Rights Division increased *significantly* every year (Smith, 1991, p. 96). Similarly, in a discussion during his Associate Attorney General confirmation hearing concerning attorney turnover in Special Litigation, Reynolds was asked to provide a summary of departures. He submitted figures for turnover in the entire Division, showing rates that did not appear out of line with that of previous administrations (*Nomination of*

William Bradford Reynolds, 1985, pp. 946–947). Congressional critics did not challenge such statistics.

Another way to deflect criticism of enforcement is to minimize the problem. "Rarely does one find the kind of blatant, inhumane, brutalization of inmates that stands out like a constitutional red flag to even the most casual observer" (Washington Council of Lawyers, 1983, p. 148, quoting William Bradford Reynolds). Rather than viewing monitoring of institutional conditions as an ongoing process, Reynolds saw it as something the federal government could someday cease to do, on one occasion asking the Section Chief, "How many more facilities were there out there before we could essentially go out of business, in other words, how much longer would CRIPA be needed?" (Interview with Arthur Peabody, 1994). To the Section Chief, such a question made as much sense as asking how much longer Title VII, or for that matter any civil rights legislation, would be needed. When good things happened in cases, credit was taken; when bad things happened, blame was avoided. For example, when the State of Illinois decided to close an institution where an investigation had just been opened, Reynolds said the decision was *because* of the Justice Department investigation (*Department of Justice Authorization for FY 83*, 1982), although there was no direct causal evidence. Likewise, William French Smith, in discussing CRIPA enforcement, said that because of Justice Department involvement, " 'Pinehurst' [sic] institution in Pennsylvania was closed" (Smith, 1991, pp. 94–95). In fact, the lawsuit involving the *Pennhurst* institution in Pennsylvania predated the Reagan Administration and CRIPA, and the Justice Department during the Reagan Administration filed a brief in the *Pennhurst* case contending that there was no constitutional right to community-based care for institutionalized residents, changing the position of the Carter Administration (Dinerstein, 1989). Contrary to Smith's assertion, the Justice Department's stance, mooted by a settlement of the case, lessened the likelihood that the institution would have been closed. On the other hand, after the fire in the Biloxi jail that killed 29 inmates, the Justice Department's press release implied that Justice had been on top of the situation, despite the fact that the Administration had blocked earlier efforts to investigate the jail as part of its ongoing prison litigation.

The Reagan Administration's policy preference toward CRIPA was one of narrow federal involvement and broad discretion toward states. The design and consistent application of its administrative strategy to achieve this preference showed a maximization of administrative control of implementation, and efforts to greatly decrease the enforcement discretion afforded careerists. The experience of CRIPA provides support for previous findings that the Reagan Administration's "efforts to decrease the policy role of civil servants were remarkably successful" (Aberbach & Rockman, 1990, p. 39). This diminished role was true within the agency, as well as in the careerists' efforts to convince Congress and stakeholders to become involved in policy review, also mirroring previous conclusions in this regard (Aberbach & Rockman, 1990).

CONGRESSIONAL INTEREST AND ACTIVITY

When Congress uses nonspecific language in statutes, it in effect is evidencing a withdrawal from concern about the particulars of enforcement (Schick, 1983, p. 161), and oversight activities on CRIPA implementation support this conclusion. Although hearings were held on Special Litigation activities, they had little impact on the overall scope of enforcement. The primary effect was to illustrate the need for the Section to maintain documentation to support its claim of active enforcement. A report by an stakeholder group charged that the Section undertook "feverish activity . . . to bolster its claims of commitment to institutional litigation" (Washington Council of Lawyers, 1983, p. 157). Nevertheless, there was no discernible increase in the number of investigations opened following the extensive congressional hearings held in late 1983, early 1984, and the spring of 1985 (*Civil Rights of Institutionalized Persons Act Hearings*, 1983; *Enforcement of Section 504 of the Rehabilitation Act*, 1983; *Civil Rights of Institutionalized Persons Act Hearings*, 1984; *Care of Institutionalized Mentally Disabled Persons*, 1985).

During the quarter including the month of the hearing on Reynolds's nomination to be Associate Attorney General, July 1985, only one investigation was opened. Although this could perhaps be attributed to Reynolds's preoccupation with preparing for the hearing, it is certainly an indication that there was little concern about congressional attention to numbers of CRIPA investigations. Litigation under CRIPA, never at a high rate, did seem to be somewhat causally related to congressional attention, with the first consent decree filed in March 1984, shortly after the first detailed hearings. Nonetheless, careerists who provided Congress with information critical of the Administration's activities ultimately concluded that not much was accomplished.

Although careerists reported that congressional staff seemed receptive and interested in their complaints, the careerists came to believe that the staff did not appreciate the issues and did not pursue them to the extent the careerists felt the subject warranted, given the seriousness of institutional deficiencies. In retrospect, some careerists feel that congressional interest in their testimony was related more to animosity toward Reynolds and the Reagan Administration, rather than to an interest in the substance of CRIPA enforcement. In many cases Congress did not scrutinize nonresponsive documentation supplied by Reynolds, suggesting that the focus of interest was primarily the demand for information, not its substance. An effort to modestly amend CRIPA died in committee.

The greatest effect of congressional attention to CRIPA enforcement is that it provided a ready-made wealth of information from which opponents could select to use against Reynolds at his confirmation hearing to be Associate Attorney General. Enforcement of CRIPA and the Voting Rights Act provided unexpected and less controversial vehicles for attacking Reynolds than did the underlying issues involving traditional civil rights enforcement. Although Reynolds ended up carrying out many of the duties of an Associate Attorney General through his appointment as Counselor to the Attorney General, the rejection of his nomination marked the end of any serious aspirations he might have had to a higher appointed office, such as the federal bench. While the rejection of his nomination had no effect on the scope of civil rights enforcement, it prevented Reynolds from receiving greater rewards for his effectiveness and loyalty to the President. The preference of Congress toward CRIPA enforcement can best be termed ambivalent to low, as little was done to change the Administration's activity through scrutiny or amendment. Ultimately, congressional attention toward CRIPA was a pawn in the larger struggle over Reagan's overall agenda.

STAKEHOLDERS

The change in institutional enforcement by the Justice Department presented a two-fold problem for stakeholders. First, they were no longer able to rely on the resources and expertise of their historic ally in institutional litigation, meaning that unless alternate resources could be identified, their activity level would fall. This also meant that they could no longer funnel information to sympathetic attorneys at Justice and have them pursue cases consistent with the stakeholders' preferences. Second, stakeholders had to expend energy and resources fighting the Justice Department itself, creating an additional adversary or even complicating settlement in cases, such as the Michigan prison suit, where the state was amenable to a broad remedial plan.

Comprehensive, critical reports such as those by the Leadership Conference on Civil Rights and the Washington Council of Lawyers examined CRIPA enforcement as part of an overall denunciation of civil rights policy, providing an impetus for congressional inquiry. The rights of institutionalized persons never commanded the level of scrutiny given to traditional civil rights matters, however, in large part due to the lack of a powerful, identifiable constituent group. As Reynolds noted, "This is an area where probably one can say that it would be hard for it to get to center stage because the constituency group are not the ones that are going to be out there marching in the streets" (Interview with William

Bradford Reynolds, 1993). Additionally, agendas varied across stakeholders—there was no unity or identity of organization, keys to effective action by policy beneficiaries (Benda & Levine, 1988). Because of the lack of a substitute for Justice Department activity, overall institutional litigation and attention decreased. "When the torch was dropped [by Justice], there was no one there to pick it up" (Interview with Section attorney).

Although stakeholders did little to alter overall CRIPA strategy, they were successful in influencing the outcome in particular cases once they were filed by Justice, such as the cases involving the Michigan prison system and mental retardation facilities in Connecticut and Massachusetts. The involvement of stakeholders in the Connecticut case prompted the only effort to amend CRIPA.

Ironically, the actions of stakeholders actually reinforced the Administration's desire to avoid litigation, because stakeholders could effectively become involved only after litigation was filed. Prolonging investigations kept the Justice Department away from the influence of activist members of the federal judiciary, such as the judge in the Michigan prison case, as well as the involvement of the stakeholders themselves. If stakeholders had been more effective in influencing policy, careerists opposing the policy internally would have been encouraged and reinforced (Benda & Levine, 1988), increasing pressure on the Administration to change.

Despite stakeholders' concern about the Administration's CRIPA enforcement, for various reasons they were unable to muster a level of activity that affected that enforcement, except for in a few, isolated cases. Where there is a presidential and congressional preference for limited implementation, and a low level of stakeholder activity, there is a high likelihood that the presidential preference will be attained.

MEDIA

The media helped bring some issues regarding CRIPA enforcement to the attention of Congress, but probably little that added to what would have been exposed by the careerists. Aspects of Reynolds' approach, such as avoiding specific policy pronouncements, meeting with critics, and relying on statutory language and caselaw interpretation, minimized the opportunity for media scrutiny. There is no indication that any reports or stories by the media galvanized public opinion in a way that affected the Administration's activities. Certainly the nature of the issues was complex and difficult to convey, and not very relevant to prevailing public concerns. Media attention was minimal.

THE COURTS

Primarily because of the *amicus* and intervention efforts of stakeholders, courts on occasion rejected the Administration's position on CRIPA issues, most notably in the Michigan prison case. Despite that court's expansion of the issues and remedies it could consider, it does not appear that that experience caused the Administration to broaden its enforcement efforts in other CRIPA cases. To the contrary, it reinforced the Administration's desire to do anything it could to avoid judicial involvement in substantive issues regarding institutional conditions and remedies, a position consistent with the Administration's view that the federal judiciary had frequently overstepped its authority with respect to institutional litigation.

CAREERISTS

Although part of the administrative strategy included how to deal with careerists, the organizational culture of Special Litigation encouraged a devoted, tenacious attitude, and few of the original careerists accepted rejection of their views without a fight. Experience in substantive legal issues was viewed by careerists as less important than having a passion for the subject matter, for experience was something that could be learned as long as some senior attorneys remained in the Section. This passion, not found in many fields of law, presented the greatest obstacle to the fulfillment of the administrative policy preference. Even Reynolds, who says in retrospect that he would do nothing differently with respect to CRIPA enforcement, concedes "The biggest problem with the institutionalized persons area, which I didn't appreciate initially and I now appreciate tremendously, is that it's very tough for someone to have that as their total agenda. I mean, this is a very depressing, thankless job, and to do it day in and day out takes a special kind of person, and I didn't factor that in nearly as much as I should have" (Interview with William Bradford Reynolds, 1993). Reynolds, however, did not indicate how consideration of the special demands on careerists would have altered his own approach to CRIPA enforcement.

The Reagan appointees arrived with a single-mindedness of purpose that matched the advocacy zeal of career civil rights attorneys. At the initial stage after the new administration arrived, there were two groups with narrow interests, energy, and strongly-held policy views, the new and the old zealots. The old zealots initially tried voice to persuade the new zealots to alter their position, believing that their preference reflected a lack of familiarity with the issues and subject matter. The Administration provided a forum for voice, but little hope of success. Relatively quickly, as their interests were implicated, the old zealots became discouraged and left. While a few attempted sabotage, reliance by the Administration on statutory language and caselaw for its policy preference provided the Administration with a legal and sometimes even moral high ground in the face of such criticism.

Policy actions that lacked a legal or moral foundation, such as the refusal to include statutory deficiencies in CRIPA cases, were too obscure to command much attention or were lost in the laundry lists of shortcomings detailed by Administration critics. When acts of sabotage surfaced, the Administration acted immediately against the actor. Coupled with a lack of policy interest by outsiders such as Congress or stakeholders groups, the action by the old zealots caused little change in overall policy. For the most part, old zealots exited quietly. As has been stated by Golden (1992, p. 45), "Reagan and Reynolds outlasted many careerists and beat those who remained at their own game of time." The greatest effect of careerist activity came in specific cases as the result of effective activity on the part of individual careerists, just as stakeholders had the most success in individual litigation.

Careerists hired after the Administration took office were selected for their policy or political ambivalence, and they generally did not actively oppose the Administration's efforts. At most, when they disagreed on issues they confined that disagreement to internal discussions about specific issues. The few experienced policy advocates hired during the Reagan Administration knew of the prevailing policy preference before they began work, and were predisposed to work with the new zealots within the system. An alliance formed among the remaining old zealots, the new careerists, and the new zealots, and this alliance of loyalists became the dominant force of activity in the Special Litigation Section.

The goal of an administration of new zealots is for the alliance that develops to pursue a policy preference as close to the administration's original preference as possible, recognizing that some moderation is inevitable. CRIPA enforcement illustrates that when the preference is for limited implementation, the administration will achieve the greatest policy success the more quickly and quietly it can cause the old zealots to leave, whether through actual exit or neglect. This minimizes the length, impact, and visibility of the zealot rivalry.

It is tempting to draw conclusions about which side was most right in its activities and which was most wrong. For the Administration, emphasizing negotiation over litigation and deferring to state-determined remedies are consistent with CRIPA's legislative history and statutory language. Disagreeing with how these policies are to be pursued in particular cases can accurately be described as a difference in enforcement philosophy. Some aspects of the Administration's enforcement efforts, however, such as refusing to include federal statutory rights in CRIPA actions, failing to follow clear precedent about remedies, and applying narrow interpretations of caselaw, appear to reflect a disregard of CRIPA, rather than just an interpretation variance. Where it is apparent that some actions clearly evidence a disregard, it is harder for opponents to believe that all decisions arise out of a difference in philosophy rather than an underlying hostility toward enforcing the law at all.

For careerists, vigorously advocating internally for a different interpretation of CRIPA and against perceived enforcement omissions is consistent with the contention that bureaucrats should employ their technical expertise and experience and serve as a check on rapid, non-incremental change. This advocacy can legitimately extend to communication with outside sources, at least where there is no disclosure of privileged information or internal documents. Some careerist actions, however, such as leaking internal documents and taking action that was contrary to explicit direction, are clearly outside the bounds of appropriate bureaucratic behavior. Just as disregarding the law in some instances makes careerists suspicious that enforcement decisions are actually due to hostility toward the law, where careerists resort to clearly unacceptable means in order to express disagreement with political direction, political appointees are skeptical of enforcement concerns careerists raise even through appropriate discourse.

This simple scorecard of right and wrong provides useful but limited insight into the effect of the administrative strategy on careerists and the overall role of careerist response in policy development. Although helping to attain their policy preferences, strategic manipulation of the bureaucracy by political appointees has pitfalls, and not just the ones usually cited by critics of an administrative approach. An administration bent on minimal enforcement of a law and reducing the activity of the bureaucracy will not be dissuaded by warnings about loss of institutional memory, continuity, or the long-range effect of its action on bureaucratic capacity. Even aside from those concerns, the policy impact of the CRIPA administrative strategy illustrates the risk to the administration itself of achieving an anti-bureaucratic policy preference.

Given that some work must be done by the agency unless the administration wishes to eliminate its function through the legislative process, the administration should want that limited work to be done as efficiently as possible, with the most enforcement directed against the worst offenders. Indeed, this seems to have been the goal of the Reagan Administration with respect to CRIPA, as reflected by the Deputy Assistant Attorney General's assertion that "we're going to do as little as possible, but everything to get it done" (Interview with Arthur Peabody, 1994, quoting Charles J. Cooper). The effect of the CRIPA strategy on careerists, and the impact of their response on enforcement, reveal that even a successful administrative strategy can have unintended and undesired consequences.

• 8 •

The Better Angels of Its Nature

"The Reagan Justice Department responded with unshakable resolve and a variety of innovative steps to bring the Nation's civil rights policies into line with the better angels of its nature" (Reynolds, 1989, p. 995).

"Internally we felt we were on the side of the angels, but we were always getting beaten up" (Interview with Section attorney).

The pursuit of its CRIPA policy preference was facilitated by the Reagan Administration's skillful application of an administrative strategy, a strategy particularly suited for vague legislation with weak, nonvocal policy beneficiaries. The career employees in the implementing agency became the proxies for the beneficiaries, and provided the strongest and most sustained opposition to the Administration's enforcement policy.

Our system of government is grounded in the belief that democracy is strengthened by spreading authority across governmental entities, and that a better whole will emerge from participation by each and even confrontation among parties. The battle between political appointees and careerists over CRIPA enforcement shows that internal confrontation is part of policy development within a branch, and can affect the struggle for consensus across branches. It is the examination of this internal confrontation that answers Rourke's question about whether there is a "fundamental element that government bureaucrats bring to the process through which public policy is made" (1992, p. 539).

In the case of CRIPA enforcement, the conflicts between political appointees and opposing careerists were exacerbated and made more emotional because each side believed it possessed superior legal and moral imperatives. Although conflict at some level is to be expected whenever there is significant policy change, the CRIPA experience is noteworthy for the widespread failure by both sides to appreciate when the activities of the other are appropriate and legitimate.

The initial impression of Reynolds is that he succeeded in attaining the Administration's policy preferences, but his legacy is mixed. The effect of the administrative strategy on career employees continues to this day, even for those who came after the Reagan Administration left office. A former Special Litigation attorney who went back to assess the Section for the Clinton transition team said he was received like "some sort of liberating army" (Interview with Section attorney). Ignoring the impact of the strategy on careerists and the ability of the office to function effectively means defining managerial success solely by whether a desired policy preference is attained: "Longer-term considerations of maintaining government machinery in good working order tend to be discounted as naive and old-fashioned. If the 'bottom line' in government management is only about policy choices, institutional considerations can be shunted aside; to the true ideologue there is no next time when the machinery must be intact to change policy directions or recalculate policy preferences. Discontinuity and the atrophy of routine governmental processes become positive virtues" (Heclo, 1983, p. 48).

Examining the ramifications of the CRIPA administrative strategy is a two-fold process: The first question concerns how the strategy affected the operation of the agency; the second, how minimizing careerist input affected the policy itself. With respect to administrative operation, although responsiveness to public opinion is claimed as a virtue by proponents of an administrative strategy, achieving a policy preference without considering whether implementation machinery is damaged may hinder an agency's ability to respond in the future. "Absent the administrative capacity to give them substance, public policies in pursuit of the public good, as articulated by elected representatives, can be no more than feeble and sterile avowals of intent" (Huddleston, 1987, p. 79). Likewise, weakening administrative capacity means diminishing long-term presidential control over the bureaucracy, which can disadvantage future like-minded administrations (Clayton, 1992). In addition to weakening the managerial structure, widespread political control of an agency can create "skepticism about the neutrality of the civil service" (Aberbach & Rockman, 1990, p. 41), casting doubt on traditional deference to agency discretion and on the legitimacy of governmental decisions. Initial policy success could thus be countermanded judicially.

If one effect of the Reagan administrative strategy was to reduce administrative capacity, this may be seen as a desirable outcome by those who support the Reagan goal to limit power in domestic agencies. The way in which administrative power was limited, however, shows how apparent administrative strategy success does not inevitably lead to attainment of the policy preference. In an atmosphere of reduced federal intrusion on states and limited resources, a policy preference of limited enforcement should mean a concentration on alleviating the worst institutional conditions, with aggressive action in a few egregious cases. This is not the way CRIPA enforcement proceeded.

The Administration avoided specific policy pronouncements and provided little guidance to the Section on how it should target institutions and conduct investigations. Attorneys had to make investigatory decisions on their own, but with no guarantee that their discretion would be taken into account in administrative review, which occurred in every instance. The result was that investigations proceeded in an "ad hoc" manner (Interview with Section attorney). Boundaries and remedies were defined on a case-by-case basis, with changes being made in the absence of specific knowledge of the subject and with little, if any, consideration of input from careerists. When clear policy statements were issued, such as those contained in the *Youngberg* memo, they seemed to careerists to be inconsistent with even Reynolds's narrow interpretation of precedent.

Once Reynolds made a determination, it was difficult for careerists to change his mind, and this became an even harder task over time with the departure of careerists experienced in policy issues and increased control by Section leadership over contacts with the front office. Many of the holdover careerists came to feel that they were essentially irrelevant; that while Reynolds might listen to or read their views, there was never a serious likelihood that he would change his position. Attorney discretion was minimized, a limitation that could not be accepted by those who had operated in a different atmosphere.

The strength and consistency of administrative control thus had several deleterious effects on the Section's ability to carry out even the limited enforcement the Administration desired. The departure of attorneys of long tenure, who had built up sources of institutional information in the field, caused their contacts to dry up, depriving the Section of a primary source of information to justify opening investigations. The turnover in attorneys resulted in a loss of institutional memory, disrupted continuity in investigations, and, in some cases, hurt the Section's credibility in negotiating with states. The ability of careerists to conduct investigations was hampered by their uncertainty of what Reynolds would find acceptable, as well as, in some cases, his personal involvement in negotiations without the knowledge of line attorneys. The involvement of the front office in every detail of investigations and litigation meant delays in proceeding, taking the management of the case out of the hands of the line attorneys and sometimes necessitating costly retours in order to get updated information. To provide some sort of structure, form consent decrees were developed that ensured structure and acceptance at the expense of institution-specific remedies. Vague language in consent decrees, used to smooth administrative review as well as to give states maximum discretion to devise their own remedies, made enforcement actions more lengthy and involved, and also increased the likelihood of stakeholder involvement and judicial oversight.

The impact of the administrative strategy on enforcement was inconsistent with an administrative goal to do less but everything possible to get it done. Just as Kraft and Vig concluded in their examination of environmental enforcement, "Reagan's administration may regulate less, but not better" (1984, p. 439). A complete review of the overall impact of the CRIPA administrative strategy would include measuring the extent to which unconstitutional institutional conditions were alleviated, a task beyond the scope of this book. Many careerists, however, felt that the overriding concern of the Administration was to limit federal involvement in state activities rather than to remedy institutional conditions, and that this misplacement of priorities disregarded the Department's obligation to enforce the law.

The second effect of the administrative strategy to be examined is what it means for policy and governance if the views and experience of careerists are not taken into account, or are even ignored. The Administration justified its civil rights enforcement by claiming an electoral mandate to reduce government. Using an administrative strategy to fulfill such a mandate is an example of how the strategy can promote political responsiveness; indeed, this is the democratic value said by Nathan to be enhanced by the use of such a strategy. Responsiveness to popular will is one democratic value; protection of minority rights is another. In many cases, careerists opposing administrative direction did so because they believed it was necessary for the protection of basic human rights, and that there were no good alternatives to federal involvement because the affected group was powerless. In essence, a special burden fell on these careerists and triggered their consciences, a burden something like the "tough agenda" acknowledged by Reynolds. This burden led to careerists acting as internal stakeholders, but with an impact that was limited because of the nature and extent of administrative control.

An administrative strategy that pursues political responsiveness to the exclusion of consideration and protection of minority rights cannot be said to be consistent with all democratic values, and adoption of such a strategy should not be lauded just because it results in apparent short-term managerial success. In the case of CRIPA implementation, the limitation on the exercise of discretion by careerists, coupled with the feeling shared by many that their expertise was not considered or desired by the political appointees, adversely affected the

Administration's policy success and minimized the protection of minority rights. This is what the policy process lost by the use of an administrative strategy that drastically reduced the participation of career civil servants. In light of the issues involved, the result could be great bodily harm or even loss of life for some of the country's most vulnerable citizens.

Trying to determine at what point to make a trade-off between federal regulation and unnecessary burdens on limited state resources is at the heart of the debate over the proper role of the federal government. Reynolds represented a change from the political appointees of the past who had let the careerists pursue civil rights enforcement as they saw fit. But the actions of the old zealots in Special Litigation illustrate that the concept of neutral competence ignores the political nature of the bureaucrats themselves. The technical policy views of the old zealots were a reflection of their own values and priorities in a way that was certainly not neutral to the values and priorities of the Administration. For many of the careerists, pressure for responsive competence resulted in a backlash of opposing political behavior, behavior that was neither responsive nor neutral. Just as there is no dichotomy between politics and administration, there is no way to construct one between responsive and neutral competence.

Clashes between careerists and political appointees bent on change are inevitable, indicative of the checks and balances of our system of government. It is disingenuous to condemn the use of an administrative strategy as unnecessarily confrontational, because confrontation of some type is a vital part of leadership in the face of opposition. But while avoiding confrontation at all costs is ineffective leadership, so also is creating conflict for the sake of conflict, without considering whether some concessions would actually help attain an administration's policy preference in the long run, as well as protecting interests that are not immediately apparent.

Therefore, individual consideration of feedback from careerists and modification of position where circumstances warrant should be added to the factors identified in previous research as important to administrative strategy success. Not all of the feedback by old zealots was detrimental to the achievement of the Administration's policy preference, yet the message conveyed by rejection of their ideas was that they themselves were irrelevant, that Reynolds and his deputies could perform the duties of the Section with only minimal involvement from anyone else. Attorneys with experience and temperament that could have helped the Section better do its limited work departed or ceased to be involved in contributing to the discussion, resulting in a loss of their talents and contacts, and causing a weakening of morale that will affect institutional capacity for years. Saboteurs could and should be dealt with harshly, but viewing all careerists as replaceable and fungible hurts the fulfillment of both immediate and long-range policy goals.

The lesson for careerists is similar. Many old zealots were unable or unwilling to recognize the legitimacy of policy direction when it differed from their own opinions, seeing any change as evisceration. Others tried to comply with retrenchment, but reached the point where they felt they were a tool of a process with which they disagreed. Careerists most successful at persuading Reynolds to adopt some of their views were those who were persistent in a nonthreatening way, and who backed up their arguments with expert opinions and analysis of precedent, rather than with appeals to emotion. Although such arguments clearly reflect the values of the careerists and cannot be viewed as neutral, presenting them in a more technical and dispassionate manner can remove the visible taint of ideological bias that sets off alarms for an appointee bent on change. Given that there is a limited amount of energy that a careerist is willing to expend before departing, it is best not to waste it by debating whether an administration is entitled to pursue its own policy preference.

As a management tool, the use of the administrative strategy in CRIPA implementation reinforces the claim that it creates "an opportunity to create a bias in favor of presidential agendas" (Durant, 1992, p. 320). How strong that bias will be depends upon the confluence of factors surrounding the policy, including the skill and determination of the primary actor in the strategy. The conclusions contained herein as to the factors involved in the success of the administrative could be well-applied to other scenarios of the strategy's use, especially where there is greater congressional or stakeholder involvement and activity. It would be helpful to include in such studies interviews with congressional, stakeholder, and media actors to determine motivations that could only be surmised in this study, and to better understand how such actors and the public can be inattentive to issues of even a sympathetic and emotional nature. Further studies could also include interviews with state and local officials concerning their views of federal activity, and their roles in facilitating the use of the strategy. Such research would be a logical progression in the studies to date of how and when an administrative strategy is best employed.

The second research implication of CRIPA concerns the more overlooked aspect of administrative presidency research—its effect across the whole of government systems. What else, aside from attainment of a policy preference, is lost or gained when an administrative strategy is successfully employed? When evaluating the use of an administrative strategy, should the definition of success be broadened to consider effects outside of the mere realization of a policy preference?

The most critical area of omission in present policy research is determining the effect of concentrating power in the executive through the use of the strategy, and how other parties can respond to that exercise of power. This research is problematic, in part because it is somewhat subjective, but also because it is difficult to define and measure the impact of an administrative strategy on entities outside of the agency involved. But if analysts of an administrative strategy continue to speak in terms of its effect on promoting democratic values, then it is time to identify and examine just what democratic values other than political responsiveness are implicated and whether they truly are promoted.

Further research should examine under what circumstances careerists help protect minority interests, and whether and how third parties fulfill that role where careerists are unable to do so. This examination could include situations where careerists are not the primary opponents to the policy, for example, where there are powerful stakeholders or influential members of Congress who can launch more effective opposition to the policy than was possible in CRIPA implementation. Such an examination would be particularly appropriate for other civil rights laws and in the area of environmental policy, where there has been substantial research into redirection of enforcement. Including an examination of enforcement by administrations subsequent to the one employing an administrative strategy in a particular case could also help reveal long-term effects of the strategy.

For many committed and idealistic civil servants, the Reagan Administration's CRIPA enforcement is an experience that evokes pain and even tears more than ten years after the fact. Their feelings are compounded by the belief held by many that the real impact of that policy was on persons who had no other source of help, and who themselves could not speak out on the harm they were facing. In light of the concern expressed by so many, it is difficult to term the Reagan Administration's strategy toward CRIPA a complete success.

Just as Heclo observed that to "the true ideologue there is no next time" when bureaucratic capacity will be desirable (1983, p. 48), the fact that an apparently successful use of the administrative strategy may trample upon minority rights is also of no real concern, as long as an immediate policy preference is realized. But where minority rights are implicated, the relatively stable administrative infrastructure can protect vulnerable groups from the adverse impact of what may even be the majority will at that time. Short-term policy success may be the desired goal for short-sighted executives, but it should not be the sole consideration for effective democratic leadership.

Appendix A: Methodological Framework

In order to assess the effectiveness of an administrative strategy, it is necessary to define what is meant by the term and determine whether such a strategy was used by the Reagan Administration. To do so, the Administration's policy preference toward CRIPA is identified by examining the statements and acts of the President and his political appointees for evidence of their ideology toward government activity of the sort authorized by CRIPA, as well as their statements and actions dealing directly with CRIPA. Once the policy preference is identified, the ways in which the Administration sought to achieve that preference are examined. If, as appears to be the case, the approach was through management of the bureaucracy rather than by legislative efforts, it can be concluded that the Administration adopted an administrative strategy.

The next avenue of inquiry is whether the use of the strategy was effective—in other words, whether the Administration achieved its policy preference (Ingraham, 1991). The objective is not to determine that the strategy was a total success or an absolute failure, but rather to evaluate the extent to which the policy that resulted from the administrative strategy resembles the presidential policy preference.

Success is measured by examining the level of CRIPA enforcement activity as well as several other indicators, including: Congressional oversight hearings led by opponents; efforts to amend CRIPA or propose legislation affecting enforcement; media coverage of enforcement activity; communications from stakeholders (defined as those who stand to gain or lose from CRIPA implementation); articles by participants and scholars; promotions of policy actors to higher positions (indicating executive approval of their performance); and elite opinions about the effectiveness of the strategy. The extent and nature of the response from those who differ with the executive preference is an especially telling factor. As stated by a Reagan appointee charged with implementing an executive preference in another area, "I knew that I was outraging the liberals, but in some ways that made my job easier. . . . It laid out the proper course more clearly. I would go up to the Senate to testify in an oversight hearing, and listen to Senators Metzenbaum and Specter rant and rave about all the awful things we were doing. That just confirmed to me that we were doing the right thing" (Hunter, 1987, p. 304).

Given that the strategy appears to be successful in achieving policy preference in a particular instance, it is helpful to identify the factors surrounding the application of the strategy that may play a role in its success. Because this study is an examination of the implementation of presidential policy preference, the same factors that have been linked to implementation success or failure can be used to analyze the use of an administrative strategy.

The organizational structure and activity of careerists are examined separately in the next section. Leaving those factors aside, the remaining factors identified as relevant to implementation success are the characteristics of the particular statute, presidential preference and the manner in which the executive branch exercises control, congressional preference and activity, stakeholder preference and activity, public opinion, the media, and the courts. For the purpose of the remaining discussion of the hypotheses, public opinion, the media, and the courts are assumed to have less of an impact on CRIPA enforcement, and are not discussed separately.

It is hypothesized that statutory vagueness facilitates the successful use of an administrative strategy, because the administration is given leeway to make its own interpretation. As to the characteristics of the statute, studies have shown that in order to reach the consensus necessary to pass legislation, specific mandates are frequently excised and replaced, if at all, by ambiguous and vague directives. Congressional proponents of strong executive enforcement may be more willing to compromise on language if they believe the administration that will be implementing it will take an expansive reading of vague directives (Hunter, 1987). Hill and Brazier (1991) found that the more the resulting legislation reflects legislative compromise, the more discretion will be given to the administrating agency. While it is true that "fuzzy" design and "fuzzy" mandates may lead to equally undefined implementation (Ingraham, 1987, p. 147), they may also lead to clear implementation that cannot be labeled as contrary to legislative intent. Administrative clarity can be the result of legislative ambiguity.

Presidential preference and the manner in which the executive branch exercises control are part of the determination of whether an administrative strategy was used. It is hypothesized that the tools available to the White House and its desire to use them aggressively also affect administrative success. In addition to the Civil Service Reform Act of 1978, in the Reagan Administration these tools included the budget, the promulgation of regulations, and ideologically consistent interpretation of vague court opinions (which like vague legislation is also generally the result of consensus and compromise). Factors peculiar to the Reagan style, such as a clear, unwavering ideology and single-mindedness in selecting nominees, also played an important role.

Aside from Administration activity, it is hypothesized that the preferences and activity level of Congress and stakeholders have the greatest effect on the success of the administrative strategy. Congressional preference and activity are determined from the legislative history, appropriation and oversight hearings, efforts to amend, statements to media, and confirmation hearings for political appointees who participated in policy implementation.

Stakeholder preference is assumed to be for full implementation of a law promoting their interests, so the key to their impact is their activity level. This is measured by examining statements about enforcement, including reports, newspaper and other articles, and congressional testimony; litigation efforts; media coverage of protests and demonstrations; and through interviews with agency attorneys and political appointees about their contacts. Although the activity of stakeholders is usually especially high in the area of civil rights (Detlefsen, 1991), CRIPA policy constituents, due to their institutionalization and disability, are less likely than traditional civil rights constituents to be outspoken in opposing civil rights policies with which they disagree (Washington Council of Lawyers, 1983). Their primary role may be to provide psychological reinforcement to careerists within the agency, who in effect then take on the role of stakeholders both because of their close identification with them and their need to maintain a position of influence within the agency.

A model was thus developed showing the likelihood of success of an administrative strategy for the combinations of preferences and activity by the president, Congress, and stakeholders. For the purpose of developing this model, the following assumptions were made:

1. Presidential policy preference is *most likely* to be realized when Congress and stakeholders have the same preference as the President, and stakeholder activity complements the implementation level supported by the President (i.e., if the President supports full implementation, the level of stakeholder activity is high; if the President supports limited implementation, the activity level is low).

2. Presidential policy preference is *least likely* to be realized when Congress has a policy preference that differs from that held by the President, and stakeholder activity is contrary to the implementation level supported by the President.

3. Stakeholder activity is *less critical* to the realization of presidential policy preference than is congressional policy agreement.

4. Achieving full implementation of a law is *more difficult* than is achieving only limited implementation.

Applying these assumptions, it is hypothesized that presidential policy preference is most likely to be realized when both Congress and the President favor limited implementation and stakeholders are inactive, because under these circumstances there will be little opposition to the realization of the policy preference. On the other hand, presidential policy preference is hypothesized to be least likely to be realized when the President favors full implementation, Congress favors limited, and stakeholders are inactive, because there will be little support for the presidential policy preference.

The second question to be addressed by this study is the effect of an administrative strategy on careerists: how they respond, and how that reaction affects an evaluation of the merits of an administrative strategy. This question has two parts: to examine what careerists do in response to an administrative strategy; and to discuss the significance of that response.

Careerists adopt a variety of approaches to counter administrative direction with which they disagree. Internally, they may voice opposition to their superiors, ask for meetings with political appointees, draft memos, limit their participation to matters on which they agree or ask to be removed from work involving certain issues, work desultorily, sabotage work, threaten departure, or actually resign. They may also take external action to effect change, such as by communicating with members of Congress or their staff, the media, and stakeholders. Memos that are drafted ostensibly for internal dissemination may be written with the hope or goal that they will fall into outside hands (Dolan, 1993).

Mild disagreement by careerists may result in only internal discussion between careerists and political appointees, leading either to acquiescence by the careerists or a slight shift in the administration's policy preference. From the administration's perspective, the greatest negative effect of disagreement by careerists occurs if their activities draw the attention of and mobilize Congress or stakeholders, who then exert pressure on the administration to alter its approach, or abandon the contention that its activities reflect the will of the people. The task for the administration is to pursue its preference in a manner that does not incite careerists to approach external actors in an effort to influence the administration, or at least limits the pressure brought by outsiders. The use of the administrative strategy to achieve a policy preference can be claimed to enhance political responsiveness if it does not produce pressure from the electorate or Congress to move in a different direction. Congress may not act for a variety of reasons, many of them having nothing to do with policy agreement (Mezey, 1989), but that inaction can be used to bolster the administration's position.

The behavior of each careerist reflects a decision reached in light of these pressures and influences, not all of which will affect every careerist. Careerist response to direction by political appointees can be used to develop a *zealot rivalry* model showing change over time in an agency that is the target of an administrative strategy (Figure 1).

The zealot rivalry model reflects the following hypotheses:

1. When there is a shift in executive preference or a new and uncharted policy to implement, careerists who view the change as inconsistent with the agency's mission will conflict with political appointees selected or instructed to adopt the new enforcement strategy.

2. Careerists hired subsequent to the adoption of and with knowledge of the new policy will be more temperate in their response to political direction, even if they have a different policy preference, because they have a different expectation about the activity of the agency, having never worked to implement the prior, differing policy.

3. Because the political appointees and the subsequently-hired careerists are operating in accordance with the presidential preference, they will be more likely to agree with each other than with the careerists hired under previous administrations (*old careerists*).

4. The old careerists will first try voice to attempt to alter what they see as a retrenchment or an undesirable shift in enforcement. Many will become discouraged and exit when their efforts do not result in a change in administrative policy.

Before the old careerists leave, there is a condition of zealot rivalry, which is an element of what Durant (1992) terms bureaucratic resistance. Rather than having only one zealot at a time (Downs, 1967), at this transitional stage there are two zealot groups with narrow interests, energy, and strongly-held policy views. The *old zealots* are those careerists hired during previous administrations who advocate the continuation of prior policies, or who see a new policy as undesirably inconsistent with the direction of a previous administration. The *new zealots* include political appointees and subsequently-hired careerists who view their job as the active pursuit of the new administration's preference. The number of old zealots who depart depends upon the distance between the two types of zealots, the intensity of the old zealots' conviction, and their mobility. The effort each makes before finally departing is in proportion to his conviction and desire for change in policy multiplied by his assessment of the probability of influencing the decision (Banfield, 1961). Although many may depart, it is hypothesized that ultimately a new alliance will form among the re-

Figure 1
Zealot Rivalry

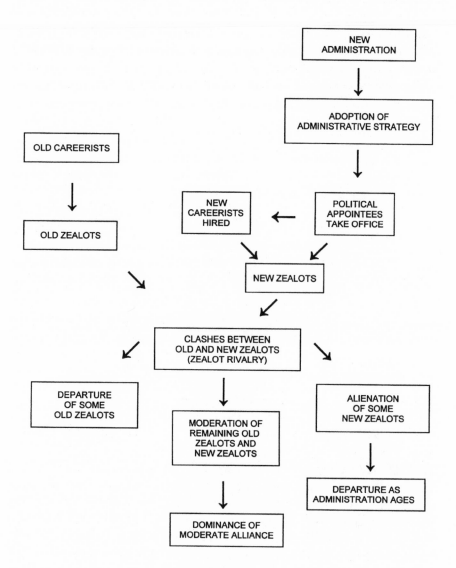

maining old and new zealots, and this alliance then becomes the dominant force of activity in the agency. Figure 1 depicts this model of zealot rivalry under a new executive seeking to administratively change policy direction, a model similar to the three-step "peeling-off" process described by Radin (1977, p. 157).

Rein and Rabinovitz (1978) identified three potentially conflicting imperatives that affect implementation: the legal imperative, or doing that which is legally required; the rational-bureaucratic imperative, or what from a bureaucratic point of view is morally correct, administratively feasible, and intellectually defensible; and the consensual imperative, or doing what is necessary to attract agreement among contending influential parties who have a stake in the outcome. The zealot rivalry model differs from that described by Rein and Rabinovitz in that it is linear, not circular, but more importantly, because it replaces the legal imperative with the more political imperative of the new zealots applying an administrative strategy.

An administration pursuing its policy preference through the use of an administrative strategy will want the activity of the ensuing alliance to closely reflect its own executive policy preference, and the administrative strategy's success can be measured by the extent to which the outputs are close to what was originally pursued. Ideally, the alliance should exactly follow the administration's original enforcement plan. Although deviation is almost certainly going to occur, it should be minimal. It is hypothesized that the nature of the policy preference an executive desires affects the type of careerist response he/she wishes to evoke. If the administration's preference is a radical departure from the agency's previous stance, the administrative strategy is *most likely* to be successful if it causes unhappy careerists to leave quickly and quietly, thereby reducing the length and visibility of the zealot rivalry and also the chance that outside actors will become involved. The desired preference is more likely to be realized, and the use of the strategy can be justified as reflecting the wishes of the electorate, because no pressure otherwise was brought to bear by third parties.

On the other hand, if the administrative preference is for increased agency activity, the alliance must be more moderate so that either some old zealots remain or there is a significant overlap between the hiring of new careerists and the departure of old zealots, in order to ensure the passing of a minimal level of institutional knowledge and enforcement continuity. For a president such as Reagan who campaigned against the bureaucracy, the departure of careerists who disagree with executive policy preferences is hypothesized to increase the likelihood that those preferences will be attained, as well as fulfill a campaign pledge to reduce the bureaucracy, at least if departed careerists are not replaced.

The remaining part of this second research question is how the response of the careerists can affect the success of the administrative strategy, examining what Heclo (1984) terms the holistic effects of government. By this, Heclo means not merely the functioning of one particular office or program, but the "cluster of interrelated parts that produces the results by which we are governed" (Heclo, 1984, p. 374). He goes on to say that attention to the whole is particularly critical in studying the Reagan presidency:

Reaganism affects governance by deploying ideologically committed appointees who not only pursue agendas but also affect organizational capacities; which helps mobilize outside groups and alliances; who then defend themselves through the courts and promote judicial activism; which then encourages members of Congress and their staffs to write legislation specifying legislative intent (or to duck the issue at hand); which then affects White House calculations as to legislative strategy—and so on and so on. Governance is a web of actions, reactions, and anticipations spread across the political landscape. Evaluations of management "success" need to take account of this larger view.

Rockman (1993) contends that part of the Reagan management approach was based on the view that because only presidential elections have issue content, the President holds a unique electoral mandate, one not shared by the unelected judiciary or even the elected Congress (p. 108). Adopting this view, only the President operates "from a truly democratic mandate" (p. 109). This mandate encourages the use of an administrative strategy, in order to better reflect the people's will. But focusing on responsiveness as the only democratic value ignores Heclo's call for a more holistic view, at least in evaluating management success.

METHODS

Research was conducted in four primary areas: public records; publications; a survey and interviews of career attorneys who worked in the agency charged with implementing CRIPA during the Reagan Administration; and interviews of supervisory attorneys, including political appointees, involved in CRIPA implementation. Public records examined include the legislative history of CRIPA; transcripts of congressional oversight, appropriation, and related hearings; annual reports on CRIPA enforcement submitted to Congress by the Department of Justice; press releases; and CRIPA litigation records in the public domain. Published materials, such as newspaper and magazine articles, law reviews, and academic publications, were reviewed for information relevant to CRIPA enforcement and careerist and constituent response.

Original data were collected through a mail survey and follow-up interviews of attorneys who worked in the Special Litigation Section of the Civil Rights Division of the Department of Justice during the Reagan Administration. The survey, reproduced in Appendix B, examined careerists' attitudes regarding the scope and nature of CRIPA enforcement; the actions they took if they disagreed with enforcement decisions; their opinions of the appropriate role of careerists faced with policy redirection; their work experiences, general and specific, prior to Special Litigation; when and why they left Special Litigation; their ideologies; and whether they voted for President Reagan. Forty-four attorneys were in the target group, of whom forty were mailed surveys (the exceptions being the author, two attorneys who could not be located, and an attorney who is deceased). Twenty-six of the forty surveys were completed and returned. All results are contained in Appendix B and some frequencies are reported in the text. Eighteen careerist and eight supervisory attorney interviews were conducted. Interviews ranged in length from thirty minutes to three hours, and were conducted between September 1993 and February 1995. In order to preserve the anonymity of their comments, quotations from non-supervisory attorneys who were interviewed are attributed in the text to "Section attorney" regardless of whether the quoted attorney was still employed in the Special Litigation Section at the time of the interview.

Appendix B: CRIPA Survey

Please circle the response which best represents the way you feel about CRIPA enforcement by the Reagan Administration. If you don't know or have no opinion leave that question blank. Feel free to write comments as space permits. Results are in **bold**.

1. Did you ever disagree with the position taken by Wm. Bradford Reynolds or one of his deputies in a CRIPA investigation or case?

     Yes-**25**
     No-**1**

2. Did you communicate your disagreement to anyone within the Department of Justice, other than line attorneys?(circle number of all that apply)

     Yes, the Assistant Attorney General-**9**
     Yes, a Deputy Assistant Attorney General(s)-**12**
     Yes, the Section Chief-**22**
     Yes, a Deputy Section Chief(s)-**17**
     Yes, other-**2** (Special assistants, other staff attorneys)
     No-**1**

3. Did you communicate your disagreement to anyone outside the Department of Justice? (circle number of all that apply)

     Yes, member(s) of Congress-**3**
     Yes, Congressional staff-**3**
     Yes, reporter(s)-**5**
     Yes, member(s) of interest group(s)-**7**
     Yes, other-**8** (advocacy groups; other federal agencies; experts; friends; family; amici; attorneys)
     No-**12**

138

4. Did you feel there were any constraints to your discussing your disagreement? (circle number of all that apply)

Yes, it could affect my performance evaluation-10
Yes, it could affect my future assignments-10
Yes, it could affect other cases of mine-7
Yes, I could affect my salary-3
Yes, I could be fired-4
Yes, the Hatch Act-0
Yes, I did not know whom to contact-1
Yes, other-5 (professional and ethical constraints; chain of command; unwilling to be identified; wouldn't have made any difference; could be "forced" out)

No-7

5. What action did you take as a result of your disagreement (circle number of all that apply)

Asked to be taken off case-4
Asked to have my name removed from pleading-6
Presented my own position in court-0
Advised sympathetic private counsel-8
Testified before Congress-2
Wrote law review or other article-2
Left Special Litigation-12
Other-8 (tried to change AAG's mind through memoranda and discussions; brought in experts; encouraged AAG to meet with advocacy groups, tour institutions, and participate in conferences; felt bad; modified pleading not in compliance with instructions and filed it; called Section Chief's attention to disagreement; retired; spoke to reporters; spoke to law students; spoke to prospective employees)

None-6

139

6. How active was the Reagan Justice Department in investigating institutions upon evidence of unconstitutional conditions?

Very active-2   Somewhat active-20   Not active-4

7. How much time was spent trying to negotiate settlement of cases?

Too much time-10   The right amount of time-8   Too little time-1

8. How specific were consent decrees?

Too specific-0   About right-5   Too general-16

9. Were staff recommendations to open investigations followed?

Almost always-0   Usually-16   Rarely-3

10. Were staff recommendations to file lawsuits or intervene in ongoing litigation followed?

Almost always-0   Usually-6   Rarely-15

11. What type of relationship did the Administration have with the states?

Too accommodating-16   About right-5   Too tough-0

12. What was the Administration's view of the constitutional rights of the institutionalized?

Too broad-1   About right-3   Too narrow-22

13. How willing was Wm. Bradford Reynolds to discuss matters with attorneys who disagreed with him?

Very willing-8   Somewhat willing-8   Not willing-6

14. How willing were Reynolds' deputies to discuss matters with staff attorneys who disagreed with them?

Very willing-6   Somewhat willing-13   Not willing-6

15. Over time, relations between Wm. Bradford Reynolds and staff attorneys...

Worsened-11   Stayed about the same-6   Improved-4

16. How many CRIPA investigations were opened?

Too many-0   The right amount-6   Too few-15

17. How many CRIPA lawsuits were filed?

Too many-1   The right amount-2   Too few-17

18. What is your opinion of the scope of CRIPA enforcement?

Too stringent-0   About right-5   Too lenient-18

19. How important is having experience in some area of civil rights of the institutionalized or disabled in conducting CRIPA investigations and litigation?

Very important-8   Helpful, but not necessary-16   Largely irrelevant-2

141

For questions 20-23, please circle the appropriate number to indicate whether you strongly agree, agree, are neutral, disagree, or strongly disagree with the following statements.

	SA	A	N	D	SD
20. The entire concept of CRIPA is based on the government's desire to ensure rights within facilities in agreement with the states involved and without resort to litigation.	3	5	1	10	5
21. Staff attorneys should accept the direction of political appointees even when they disagree with it.	2	9	2	7	4
22. It would be hard for me to enforce policies I do not believe in.	12	11	2	1	0
23. Staff attorneys who disagree with the policy direction of political appointees should leave the agency.	4	10	5	7	0

24. When did you begin working in the Special Litigation Section?

Before 1/77-3   7/84-12/84-2
1/77-1/81-6   1/85-6/85-0
2/81-6/81-0   7/85-12/85-1
7/81-12/81-3   1/86-6/86-0
1/82-6/82-0   7/86-12/86-0
7/82-12/82-0   1/87-6/87-0
1/83-6/83-2   7/87-12/87-1
7/83-12/83-6   1/88-6/88-1
1/84-6/84-1   7/88-1/89-0

142

25. How were you hired into the Special Litigation Section?

Attorney General's Honors Program-10
Transfer within Justice Department-2
Sent application-13
Referred by someone in Justice Department-1

26. Before coming to the Special Litigation Section, how much prior legal experience did you have in each of the following...

	>10 Years	5-10 Years	2-5 Years	<2 Years	None
a. Law firm/Private	0	1	5	3	14
b. Government	1	2	5	2	13
c. Public interest group	0	2	1	4	15
d. Law school faculty	0	0	0	0	20
e. Judicial clerkship	0	0	0	3	17
f. Other	0	1	1	3	13

27. Before coming to the Special Litigation Section, what prior experience did you have in the area of civil rights of the disabled or institutionalized? (circle all that apply)

I had legal experience-9
I was a member of an interest group-4
I am disabled-2
I had a family member who was disabled-2
I had published articles on this topic-5
I had a degree in a related area-3
None-10
Other-5 (had taken related courses; internship; law school clinic; agency employment; volunteer work)

143

28. If you still work in the Special Litigation Section, skip to Question 32. If you left Special Litigation, indicate the month and year of your departure.

1/81-6/81-0	1/84-6/84-3	1/87-6/87-4
7/81-12/81-2	7/84-12/84-0	7/87-12/87-1
1/82-6/82-1	1/85-6/85-0	1/88-6/88-1
7/82-12/82-2	7/85-12/85-2	7/88-12/88-1
1/83-6/83-1	1/86-6/86-1	1/89-1/93-1
7/83-12/83-3	7/86-12/86-0	Still there-3

29. Why did you leave the Special Litigation Section? (circle number of all that apply)

I wanted to earn a higher salary-3
I wanted to do more litigation-9
I wanted to do less litigation-0
I moved out of the D.C. area-6
I wanted to leave the practice of law-0
I wanted to work in a different area of law-11
I disagreed with the Administration's position on CRIPA-15
I disagreed with the Administration's position on other laws or policies-13
Other-9 (incompetence of Section leadership; wanted to teach; wanted to go into private practice; attractive opportunity; unfairly
facing disciplinary action; too much travel; professional disagreement with supervisor; time to move on)

30. Which of the above were the most important reasons for your departure?

Most Important	Second Most Important
Salary-1	Salary-1
More litigation-3	More litigation-3
Leave DC-2	Different law-5
Different law-2	Disagree-CRIPA-3
Disagree-CRIPA-8	Disagree-Other-5
Disagree-Other-3	Other-5
Other-4	

144

31. Did you communicate your reason(s) for leaving to anyone in a supervisory position at Justice? (circle number of all that apply)

Yes, the Assistant Attorney General-5
Yes, a Deputy Assistant Attorney General(s)-4
Yes, the Section Chief-18
Yes, a Deputy Section Chief(s)-12
Other-3 (line attorneys; friends; everybody)
No-3

32. Which best describes your political ideology?

Very Conservative	Conservative	Moderate	Liberal	Very Liberal
1	4	6	9	6

33. Did you vote for Ronald Reagan for President?

Yes, in both 1980 and 1984	Yes, in 1980 only	Yes, in 1984 only	No
2	0	2	21

34. Would you be willing to be interviewed for this study?

Yes	No
20	6

Appendix C: Summary of CRIPA Enforcement: 5/80–1/89

Ada County Jail, Boise, ID
> Type of facility: Jail
> Investigation opened: 1/6/83
> Findings issued: 4/18/84
> Settlement agreement entered: 5/23/85. Will monitor.
> FY 86: Continuing to monitor.
> Consent decree dismissed: 12/18/86. First CRIPA consent decree to be completed and terminated.

Agana Adult Correctional Facility, Agana, Guam
> Type of facility: Prison
> Investigation opened: 5/12/86
> Findings issued: 8/11/87
> FY 88: Under review.

Agana Lock-Up, Agana, Guam
> Type of facility: Jail
> Investigation opened: 5/12/86
> FY 87: Jail closed for renovation.

Agana Mental Health Unit, Agana, Guam
> Type of facility: Prison
> Investigation opened: 5/12/86
> Findings issued: 8/11/87
> FY 88: Under review.

Atascadero State Hospital, Atascadero, CA
> Type of facility: MH

Investigation opened: 7/1/82

FY 83: Investigation continuing.

Findings issued: 5/1/84

FY 85: Negotiations pending.

FY 86: Negotiations have been unfruitful. Facility has been retoured, further action pending.

FY 87: Monitoring state's progress.

FY 88: Continuing to monitor.

Attica Prison, Attica, NY

Type of facility: Prison

Investigation opened: 11/14/80

Findings issued and investigation closed: 9/2/82 ("conditions not violations of the sort Congress intended to be redressed under CRIPA").

Bedford County Jail, Shelbyville, TN

Type of facility: Jail

Investigation opened: 3/5/84

Findings issued: 8/29/84

Consent decree entered: 1/17/85. Will monitor.

FY 86: County will construct new facility.

FY 87: Monitoring construction progress.

FY 88: Inmates moved to new jail.

Belle Chasse School (Metropolitan Developmental Center), Belle Chasse, LA

Type of facility: MR

Investigation opened: 11/30/84

Findings issued and State refused consent decree: 4/86.

Reinvestigated: 6/86

Updated findings issued: 8/22/86

Lawsuit filed: 1/5/87

Consent decree filed: 7/23/87

FY 88: Tours indicated improvement. Monitoring.

Benton Services Center Nursing Home, Benton, AK

Type of facility: Nursing home

Investigation opened: 3/23/81

FY 82: Investigation pending.

Findings issued: 5/24/83

Investigation closed: 9/17/84 ("constitutionally adequate levels of care and treatment").

Broadview Developmental Center, Broadview Heights, OH (see also Cleveland and Warrensville)

Type of facility: MR

Investigation opened: 4/1/86

FY 87: Investigation continuing.
Findings issued: 11/20/87

Buffalo Psychiatric Center, Buffalo, NY
Type of facility: MH
Investigation opened: 1/3/86
Findings issued: 2/27/87
Lawsuit filed: 2/5/88. State had refused to negotiate.

California Medical Facility, Vacaville, CA
Type of facility: Prison
Investigation opened: 3/7/85
FY 86: Investigation continuing.
Findings issued: 1/6/87
Supplemental findings issued: 7/22/88. Facility retoured.

Central Islip Psychiatric Center, Long Island, NY (see also Kings Park and Pilgrim)
Type of facility: MH
Investigation opened: 9/30/87
FY 88: Investigation continuing.

Central State Hospital, Indianapolis, IN
Investigation opened: 10/8/83
Lawsuit filed and consent decree entered: 3/16/84. Will monitor. (First MH consent decree)
FY 85: Continuing to monitor
FY 86: Continuing to monitor
FY 87: Deficiencies exist. Will continue to monitor, and consider other remedies.
FY 88: Deficiencies still exist. Will revisit.

Cleveland Developmental Center, Garfield Heights, OH (see also Broadview and Warrensville)
Type of facility: MR
Investigation opened: 4/1/86
FY 87: Investigation continuing.
Findings issued: 11/20/87. Facility closed 4/88.

Clinton Correctional Facility, Dannemora, NY
Type of facility: Prison
Investigation opened: 6/20/84
FY 85: Investigation continuing.
FY 86: Investigation continuing.
Investigation closed: 4/22/87. ("Conditions there do not rise to the level of constitutional deprivations.")

Cook County Jail, Chicago, IL
Type of facility: Jail
FY 82: Opened investigation under CRIPA due to court's remand in *United States v. Elrod.*

FY 83: No further action warranted (private consent decree in another case).
Will continue to monitor.
FY 84: Investigation closed.

Cornwell Heights Youth Development Center, Ben Salem, PA
Type of facility: Juvenile
Investigation opened: 12/15/80
Findings issued: 3/18/82
FY 83: Further investigation unwarranted (state has made substantial progress).
FY 84: Investigation closed.

Creedmoor Psychiatric Center, Queens, NY
Type of facility: MH
Investigation opened: 2/4/88
FY 88: Suit for access filed. Settled by stipulation; investigation continues.

Crittenden County Jail, Marion, AR
Type of facility: Jail
Investigation opened: 11/7/86
Findings issued: 6/1/87
FY 88: Consent decree negotiated, but no one will sign for county. Examining
options.

Cummins Unit, Arkansas Department of Corrections
Type of facility: Prison
Investigation opened: 9/18/85
FY 86: Investigation continuing.
FY 87: Investigation continuing.
FY 88: Investigation continuing.

Dauphin County Prison, Harrisonburg, PA
Type of facility: Jail
Investigation opened: 10/15/80.
Investigation closed: 8/4/81 (No further action warranted).

Deer Island House of Corrections, Boston, MA
Type of facility: Prison
Investigation opened: 12/3/80
Findings issued: 5/18/82. Further investigation unwarranted due to private law-
suit. Will continue to monitor.

Dixon Development Center, Dixon, IL
Type of facility: MR
Investigation opened: 7/13/81
Governor announced facility to close: 2/17/82
FY 82: Investigation continuing.
Investigation closed: 10/26/82 (facility closed).

Eastern Oregon Training Center, Pendleton, OR
    Type of facility: MR
    Investigation opened: 11/19/85
    Findings issued: 7/28/86
    FY 87: Retoured, follow-up letter. Proposed consent decree sent.
    FY 88: Attempted to arrange retours; state resisted citing burden of prepar-
        ing for Fairview litigation. Investigation continuing.

East Louisiana State Hospital, Jackson, LA
    Type of facility: MH
    Investigation opened: 11/5/80
    Findings issued: 3/8/82
    FY 83: Satisfied with progress—will continue to monitor.
    Investigation closed: 9/26/84 ("no flagrant or egregious conditions of confine-
        ment that deprive residents of their constitutional rights presently exist")

Ebensburg Center, Ebensburg, PA
    Type of facility: MR
    Investigation opened: 8/8/86
    FY 87: Finalizing investigation.
    Findings issued: 11/19/87

Edgemoor Geriatric Hospital, Santee, CA
    Type of facility: Nursing home
    Investigation opened: 5/30/86
    Findings issued: 2/5/87
    FY 88: Retour showed improvements. Will allow reasonable time to complete
        them.

Elgin Mental Health Center, Elgin, IL (see also Manteno)
    Type of facility: MH
    Investigation opened: 2/17/83
    FY 84: Investigation continuing.
    Findings issued: 12/13/84
    Notified of deficiencies: 3/6/86
    Lawsuit and consent decree filed: 10/3/86. Will monitor.
    FY 88: Monitoring.

Ellisville State School, Ellisville, MS
    Type of facility: MR
    Investigation opened: 9/11/85
    Findings issued: 3/25/86
    FY 87: Negotiating productively.
    FY 88: Negotiating terms of proposed decree.

Embreeville Center, Embreeville, PA
    Type of facility: MR
    Investigation opened: 9/11/86

FY 87: Investigation continuing.
FY 88: Investigation continuing.

Enid State School, Enid, OK
Type of facility: MR
Investigation opened: 4/9/82
Report of findings: 5/23/83
FY 83: Will monitor adequacy of improvements.
FY 84: Monitoring.
Investigation closed: 1/5/85 (conditions "no longer constitutionally inadequate").

Essex County Jail, NJ
Type of facility: Jail
Investigation opened: 4/7/82
Investigation closed: 8/23/82 (consent decree reached in private lawsuit).

Essex County Youth House, Newark, NJ
Type of facility: Juvenile
Investigation opened: 1/6/86
Findings issued: 7/23/86.
FY 87: Trying to negotiate.
Lawsuit and consent decree filed: 12/3/87. Compliance tour indicated continued serious problems.

Fairview Training Center, Salem, OR
Type of facility: MR
Investigation opened: 5/13/83
FY 84: Investigation continuing.
Findings issued: 3/15/85
Lawsuit filed: 7/28/86. (first contested MR lawsuit).
FY 87: Discovery underway. Court denied motion to intervene filed by residents.
FY 88: Active discovery.

Feliciana Forensic Facility, Jackson, LA
Type of facility: MH
Investigation opened: 11/5/80
Findings issued (intent to intervene): 4/9/82
Intervened (*Davis v. Henderson*): 5/28/82 (first CRIPA intervention).
FY 83: Negotiations to resolve lawsuit pending
Consent decree entered: 12/2/83. Will monitor.
FY 87: Reviewing compliance information.
FY 88: Reviewing compliance information.

Folsom State Prison, Represa, CA
Type of facility: Prison
Investigation opened: 8/25/80
Findings issued: 4/3/84

FY 84: Investigation continuing.

Investigation closed: 3/18/85 (Because of private litigation, and the appointment of a monitor in that case to evaluate compliance, "appropriate steps were being taken to protect inmates' constitutional rights.")

Fort Stanton Hospital and Training School, Fort Stanton, NM
Type of facility: MR
Investigation opened: 12/18/84
Findings issued: 12/24/85
Consent decree rejected by state.
Lawsuit filed: 8/8/86
FY 87: Litigation stayed pending state's remedial efforts.
FY 88: Tours indicated progress.
Lawsuit dismissed: 12/12/88

Golden Grove Correctional Institution, St. Croix, VI
Type of facility: Prison
Investigation opened: 5/28/85
Findings issued: 1/23/86
Lawsuit and consent decree filed: 11/21/86
FY 88: Motion to show cause filed. Tour indicated continued deficiencies. Court to order United States to draw up remedial plan.

Graterford State Prison, Graterford, PA
Type of facility: Prison
Investigation opened: 4/26/83
Letter about lack of access: 8/3/83
Findings issued and investigation closed: 4/26/84 ("conditions of confinement do not violate the constitutional rights of inmates").

Great Oaks Center, Silver Spring, MD
Type of facility: MR
Investigation opened: 11/18/86
FY 88: Investigation continuing.

Grenada County Jail, Grenada, MS
Type of facility: Jail
Investigation opened: 11/1/82
Investigation closed: 2/22/84 ("conditions at the jail do not rise to the level of constitutional violations").

Harrison County Jails, Gulfport & Biloxi, MS
Type of facility: Jail
Investigation opened: 8/19/82
FY 83: Investigation continuing.
FY 84: Investigation continuing.
Investigation closed: 1/28/85 ("no unreasonable risks"; "commitment of the

Sheriff's Department to operate the jails in conformity with constitutional principles")

Hazelwood Intermediate Care Facility, Louisville, KY
Type of facility: MR
Investigation opened: 11/29/82
Investigation closed: 8/27/84 (areas of concern "are not flagrant or egregious conditions of confinement that deprive residents of their constitutional or federal statutory rights").

Hinds County Detention Center, Hinds County, MS
Type of facility: Jail
Investigation opened: 3/11/86
6/26/86: Chancery Court (on own motion) enjoined further confinement in jail. In light of this, investigation is on hold, but will continue to monitor.
Findings issued: 11/4/86
Investigation closed: 4/22/87 ("We are now satisfied that the [facility] is no longer confining . . . persons without adequate safeguards.")

Howe Developmental Center, Tinley Park, IL
Type of facility: MR
Investigation opened: 4/18/86
FY 87: Investigation continuing.
Findings issued: 5/20/88. Will determine course of action after State implements new initiatives.

Jackson Special Hospital, Jackson, LA
Type of facility: Prison
Investigation opened: 6/16/82
FY 83: Investigation continuing.
FY 84: Investigation closed.

Jefferson County Jail, Steubenville, OH
Type of facility: Jail
Investigation opened: 12/16/85
Findings issued: FY 86 (no date given).
Lawsuit filed: 4/9/87
Consent decree entered: 4/10/87
FY 88: Monitoring.

Kalamazoo Regional Psychiatric Hospital, Kalamazoo, MI
Type of facility: MH
Investigation opened: 2/5/85
Findings issued: 3/13/86
Lawsuit and consent decree filed: 9/16/87
FY 88: Monitoring compliance and reviewing State's plan of implementation.

Kansas State Penitentiary, Lansing, KS
> Type of facility: Prison
> Investigation opened: 2/18/86
> Findings issued: 6/3/87
> FY 88: Retoured. Monitoring private action to determine how to proceed.

Kings Park Psychiatric Center, Long Island, NY (see also Central Islip and Pilgrim)
> Type of facility: MH
> Investigation opened: 9/30/87
> FY 88: Investigation continuing.

Las Vegas Medical Center, Las Vegas, NM (New Mexico State Hospital)
> Type of facility: MH
> Investigation opened: 1/15/86
> Findings issued: 10/29/86
> Investigation closed: 4/25/88 ("conditions . . . no longer violated the constitutional rights of residents").

Logansport State Hospital, Logansport, IN (see also Central State)
> Type of facility: MH
> Investigation opened: 6/16/82
> FY 83: Investigation continuing.
> Lawsuit filed and consent decree entered: 4/6/84. Will monitor.
> FY 85: Continuing to monitor.
> FY 86: Continuing to monitor.
> FY 87: Deficiencies exist. Will continue to monitor, and consider other remedies.
> FY 88: Deficiencies still exist. Will revisit.

Los Angeles County Jails, Los Angeles, CA
> Type of facility: Jail
> Investigation opened: 10/21/85
> Investigation closed: 5/5/86. ("Jails were being operated in conformity with constitutional requirements. . . . [A]dditional plans of correction . . . convinced us that further action by the Department is not warranted.")

Los Angeles County Juvenile Halls, Los Angeles, CA
> Type of facility: Juvenile
> Investigation opened: 3/28/85
> Lawsuit filed (denial of access): 3/27/86
> Injunction against facility issued: 5/9/86 (reported at *United States v. Los Angeles*, 635 F. Supp. 588 (C.D. Cal. 1986).
> FY 86: Investigation continuing.
> FY 87: Investigation continuing.
> Findings issued: 10/28/87. Retoured.

Los Lunas Hospital and Training School, Los Lunas, NM
> Type of facility: MR

Investigation opened: 1/21/87
Findings issued: 9/12/88

Manchester Youth Development Center, Manchester, NH
Type of facility: Juvenile
Investigation opened: 5/11/82
FY 83: Investigation continuing.
Investigation closed: 8/30/84 ("substantial improvements" will result in the near future).

Manteno Mental Health Center, Manteno, IL (see also Elgin)
Type of Facility: MH
Investigation opened: 4/9/82
FY 83: Investigation continuing.
FY 85: Investigation continuing.
Findings issued: 12/13/84
Investigation closed: 3/6/86 (facility closed).

Michigan State Prison System, Ionia, Jackson, Marquette, MI
Type of facility: Prison
Investigation opened: 10/9/81
Findings issued: 11/1/82
Consent decree entered: 7/16/84. Will monitor.
FY 85: Continuing to monitor.
FY 86: Continuing to monitor.
FY 87: Continuing to monitor.
FY 88: Monitoring.

Missouri Training Center for Men, Moberly, MO
Type of facility: Prison
Investigation opened: 12/9/85
FY 87: Investigation continuing. Evaluating impact of pending private lawsuit.
Investigation closed: 10/5/87 Concerns were addressed in three private cases.

Montgomery Developmental Center, Huber Heights, OH
Type of facility: MR
Investigation opened: 9/10/85
FY 86: Investigation continuing.
Findings issued: 3/5/87
FY 88: Retour showed improvements. Investigation continuing.
Investigation closed: 11/1/88

Napa State Hospital, Imola, CA
Type of facility: MH
Investigation opened: 7/17/85
Findings issued: 5/28/86
FY 87: Monitoring state's progress.
FY 88: Continuing to monitor.

Newark City Jail, Newark, NJ
>   Type of facility: Jail
>   Investigation opened: 4/7/82
>   Findings issued: 7/13/82
>   FY 83: Proposed consent decree sent to state.
>   Lawsuit filed: 2/2/84.
>   Trial conducted: 8/84–9/84
>   Settlement agreement entered: 7/15/85. Special Masters will monitor compliance, as will DOJ.
>   FY 86: Continuing to monitor.
>   FY 87: Contempt motion (denial of access) filed. Access then granted. Deficiencies found. Will continue to monitor.
>   FY 88: Motion to show cause filed 2/2/88. Stayed pending negotiations.

Northville Regional Psychiatric Hospital, Northville, MI
>   Type of facility: MH
>   Investigation opened: 11/15/82
>   FY 84: Investigation continuing.
>   Findings issued: 2/19/85
>   Consent decree: 8/7/86
>   FY 87: Monitoring.
>   FY 88: Reviewing compliance.

Oahu Community Correctional Center, Honolulu, HI
>   Type of facility: Prison
>   Investigation opened: 6/10/82
>   Findings issued (refusal of access): 8/24/82
>   Lawsuit filed (access): 3/4/83 (first non-intervention lawsuit).
>   Lawsuit dismissed (failure to follow procedural requirements-5/10/83).
>   Revised findings issued: 7/8/83
>   FY 84: New investigation continuing.
>   Findings issued: 12/18/84. (Closed investigation at Halawa High Security Facility—"no deficiencies rose to a level which violates inmates' constitutional rights).
>   Investigation closed: 6/5/86 (An "adequate remedial plan of compliance" is in effect as a result of DOJ investigation and settlement of private lawsuit brought by ACLU.)

Orlando Sunland Training Center, Orlando, FL
>   Type of facility: MR
>   Investigation opened: 6/24/82
>   FY 82: Will close investigation due to private consent decree

Ossining Correctional Facility, Ossining, NY (Sing Sing)
>   Type of facility: Prison
>   Investigation opened: 6/20/83
>   FY 84: Investigation continuing.

FY 85: Investigation continuing.
Investigation closed: 8/13/86 ("absence of any continuing constitutional violation").

Pauls Valley State School, Pauls Valley, OK
Type of facility: MR
Investigation opened: 4/9/82
Findings issued: 5/23/83
FY 83: Will monitor adequacy of improvements.
FY 84: Monitoring.
FY 85: Monitoring.
FY 86: Closed investigation 5/2/86. ("[V]oluntary remedial measures served to bring conditions . . . into compliance with constitutional requirements.").

Pilgrim Psychiatric Center, Long Island, NY (see also Central Islip and Kings Park)
Type of facility: MH
Investigation opened: 9/30/87
FY 88: Investigation continuing.

Preston School of Industry, Ione, CA
Type of facility: Juvenile
Investigation opened: 12/11/85
Findings issued: 9/10/86
FY 87: Continuing negotiations.
FY 88: Continuing negotiations.

Rosewood Center, Owings Mills, MD
Type of facility: MR
Investigation opened: 11/7/80
Findings issued: 2/19/82
FY 83: Reviewing plan of correction.
FY 84: Investigation continuing.
Consent decree entered: 1/17/85. Will monitor.
FY 86: Continuing to monitor. Determined not in compliance. Entered into a stipulation on 6/4/86, which included a plan for upgrade. State still not in compliance. Considering options.
FY 87: Deficiencies still exist. Will evaluate course of action.
FY 88: Amended consent decree. Monitoring.
FY 89: Stipulation filed with court.

Sandusky County Jail, Fremont, OH
Type of facility: Jail
Investigation opened: 5/15/86
Investigation closed: 7/23/87 (many improvements, settlement of a private lawsuit, plans for a new jail).

San Francisco Youth Guidance Center, San Francisco, CA
Type of facility: Juvenile

Investigation opened: 3/28/85
Findings issued: 8/26/86
Follow-up findings letter: 7/21/87
FY 88: Retoured. Will revisit in six months.

Santana v. Collazo (D.P.R.)
Type of facility: Juvenile
Intervention filed: 1/27/81
DOJ's post-trial brief and proposed findings filed: 11/2/81
Order issued: 2/17/82

Santa Rita Jail, Pleasanton, CA
Type of facility: Jail
Investigation opened: 9/17/86
Findings issued: 8/11/87
FY 88: Monitoring and negotiating.

South Beach Psychiatric Center, Staten Island, NY
Type of facility: MH
Investigation opened: 2/22/84
Findings issued and investigation closed: 9/21/84 ("current conditions met
    constitutional minima").

Southbury Training School, Southbury, CT
Type of facility: MR
Investigation opened: 5/1/84
Findings issued: 9/11/85
Lawsuit and consent decree filed: 7/25/86
Consent decree entered: 12/22/86. Delay due to efforts of Connecticut
    Protection and Advocacy and Home and School Association of Southbury
    Training School to participate in negotiations or intervene.
FY 88: Tours indicated deficiencies. Monitoring.

South Carolina State Hospital, Columbia, SC
Type of facility: MH
Investigation opened: 10/6/83
Findings issued: 11/23/84
Settlement agreement signed: 6/24/86
FY 87: Monitoring.
FY 88: Monitoring.

South Florida State Hospital, Hollywood, FL
Type of facility: MH
Investigation opened: 3/23/81
Findings issued and remedial plans received: 8/5/81; investigation on hold.
FY 82: Monitoring progress.
FY 83: Reviewing status report.
Investigation closed: 6/12/84 ("areas of concern did not reflect the type of

flagrant and egregious conditions Congress intended us to address under the Act").

Spring Grove Hospital Center, Catonsville, MD
  Type of facility: MH
  Investigation opened: 8/18/82
  FY 83: Investigation continuing (letter sent 11/3/82: intent to file due to lack of access).
  Investigation closed: 9/18/84 ("provide(s) constitutionally adequate care").

Talledega County Jail, Talledega, AL
  Type of facility: Jail
  Investigation opened: 8/27/82
  FY 83: Advised county that complaint would be filed (access and other matters—7/7/83).
  FY 84: Investigation continuing.
  Settlement agreement entered: 9/17/85. Will monitor.
  FY 86: Continuing to monitor.
  FY 87: Deficiencies found. Will continue to monitor.
  FY 88: Tours indicated continued deficiencies. Time for complying with decree extended.

Tutwiler Prison for Women, Wetumpka, AL
  Type of facility: Prison
  Investigation opened: 7/3/84
  FY 85: Investigation continuing.
  Findings issued: 3/24/86
  Lawsuit filed: 1/6/87. Stayed by court 5/4/87, pending resolution of a private lawsuit, which was resolved 8/27/87. U.S. case dismissed 9/14/87 in light of comprehensive private lawsuit settlement.

Vermont State Hospital, Waterburg, VT
  Type of facility: MH
  Investigation opened: 12/17/85
  Investigation closed: 5/8/86 ("generally adequate programs . . . that do not deprive VSH residents of any federal constitutional rights").

Warrensville Developmental Center, Warrensville, OH (see also Broadview and Cleveland)
  Type of facility: MR
  Investigation opened: 4/1/86
  FY 87: Investigation continuing.
  Findings issued: 11/20/87

Washington County Jail, Washington County, Mississippi
  Type of facility: Jail
  Investigation opened: 10/14/87. Problem appears to be resolved. Will soon close investigation.

Westboro State Hospital, Westboro, MA
    Type of facility: MH
    Investigation opened: 9/10/85
    Findings issued: 12/1/86
    FY 87: Settlement negotiations pending.
    FY 88: Settlement discussions continue.
    Findings reissued: 10/88

Western State Correctional Institution, Pittsburgh, PA
    Type of facility: Prison
    Investigation opened: 12/12/80
    Findings issued: 8/5/81
    FY 82: Investigation closed based on review of state's remedial plans.

West Virginia Industrial School for Boys, Pruntytown, WV
    Type of facility: Juvenile
    Investigation opened: 2/24/81
    Findings issued: 3/18/82
    FY 83: Further investigation is unwarranted. State will provide periodic reports on corrective measures.
    FY 84: Investigation closed.

Wheat Ridge Regional Center, Wheat Ridge, CO
    Type of facility: MR
    Investigation opened: 12/16/83
    Findings issued: 12/7/84
    Lawsuit and settlement agreement filed: 7/10/86
    FY 87: Monitoring.
    FY 88: Monitoring.

Winfield State Hospital and Training School, Winfield, KS
    Type of facility: MR
    Investigation opened: 9/30/87
    Findings issued: 7/27/88. Will reevaluate in six months.

Wisconsin Prison System
    Type of facility: Prison
    Investigation opened: 12/3/80
    Findings issued: 6/17/82
    Investigation closed: 3/3/83 ("while some aspects of their response were troubling, we concluded that . . . the system did not merit further action").

Worcester State Hospital, Worcester, MA
    Type of facility: MH
    Investigation opened: 10/4/82
    Findings issued: 4/23/84
    Lawsuit filed: 2/11/85 (first contested MH lawsuit). Discovery pending.
    FY 86: Discovery nearing completion.

Settlement agreement entered 8/25/87 after week-long trial. Will monitor.

FY 88: Serious compliance problems necessitate considering filing a motion for contempt.

FY 89: Motion to show cause filed. (Ultimately lost by U.S., 890 F.2d 507 (1st Cir. 1989)).

Ypsilanti Psychiatric Hospital, Ypsilanti, MI

Type of facility: MH

Investigation opened: 11/18/83

Findings issued: 2/19/85

Consent decree: 8/7/86

FY 87: Monitoring.

FY 88: Reviewing compliance.

References

Aberbach, J. D., & Rockman, B. A. (1990). What has happened to the U.S. Senior Career Service? *The Brookings Review,* 8, 35–41.

_____ . (1993). *Civil servants and policy makers: Neutral or responsive competence?* Paper presented at the annual meeting of the American Political Science Association, Washington, DC.

Aberbach, J. D., Rockman, B. A., & Copeland, R. M. (1990). From Nixon's problem to Reagan's achievement: The federal executive reexamined. In L. Berman (Ed.), *Looking Back on the Reagan Presidency* (pp. 175–194). Baltimore: Johns Hopkins University Press.

Alexander, E. (1984). Justice Department retreats: The Michigan case. *The National Prison Project Journal,* 1, 4–6.

Amaker, N. C. (1988). *Civil Rights and the Reagan Administration.* Washington, DC: Urban Institute Press.

Aman, A. C., Jr. (1992). *Administrative Law in a Global Era.* Ithaca: Cornell University Press.

American Civil Liberties Union. (1984). *In Contempt of Congress and the Courts—The Reagan Civil Rights Record.* Washington, DC: ACLU.

Anderson, M. (1990). *Revolution: The Reagan Legacy.* Stanford: Hoover Institution Press.

Antonelli, L. M. (1984, June). J. Harvie Wilkinson's judgment day. *Commonwealth,* 51, 44–48, 60–62.

Authorization, Legislation and Oversight of the U.S. Department of Justice, Part 4 (Civil Rights Division and INS): Hearing Before the Senate Judiciary Committee, 100th Cong., 1st Sess. (1987).

Authorization Request for the Civil Rights Division of the Department of Justice: Hearings Before the Subcommittee on Civil and Constitutional Rights of the House Committee on the Judiciary, 97th Cong., 2d Sess. (1982).

Authorization Request for the Civil Rights Division of the Department of Justice: Hearings Before the Subcommittee on Civil and Constitutional Rights of the House Committee on the Judiciary, 99th Cong., 1st Sess. (1985).

Authorization Request for the Civil Rights Division of the Department of Justice: Hearings Before the Subcommittee on Civil and Constitutional Rights of the House Committee on the Judiciary, 99th Cong., 2d Sess. (1986).

Authorization Request for the Civil Rights Division of the Department of Justice: Hearings Before the Subcommittee on Civil and Constitutional Rights of the House Committee on the Judiciary, FY 88, 100th Cong., 1st Sess. (1987).

Ball, H., & Greene, K. (1985). The Reagan Justice Department. In T. Yarbrough (Ed.), *The Reagan Administration and Human Rights* (pp. 1–28). New York: Praeger.

Ban, C., & Ingraham, P.W. (1990). Short-Timers: Political appointee mobility and its impact on political and career relations in the Reagan administration. *Administration and Society, 22*, 106–124.

Banfield, E. C. (1961). *Political Influence*. New York: Free Press of Glencoe.

Bardach, E. (1977). *The Implementation Game: What Happens After a Bill Becomes a Law?* Cambridge, MA: MIT Press.

Battle v. Anderson, 564 F.2d 388 (10th Cir. 1977).

Benda, P. M., & Levine, C. H. (1988). Reagan and the bureaucracy: The bequest, the promise, and the legacy. In C. O. Jones (Ed.), *The Reagan Legacy: Promise and Performance* (pp. 102–142). Chatham, NJ: Chatham House.

Brownstein, R. (1985, July 13). Ambiguous victory. *National Journal*, p. 1654.

Brownstein, R., & Easton, N. (1982). *Reagan's Ruling Class: Portraits of the President's Top One Hundred Officials*. New York: Pantheon.

Bullock, C. S. III. (1984b). Equal education opportunity. In C. S. Bullock III & C. M. Lamb (Eds.), *Implementation of Civil Rights Policy* (pp. 55–92). Monterey, CA: Brooks/Cole.

Bullock, C. S. III, Anderson, J., & Brady, D. (1983). *Public Policy in the Eighties*. Monterey, CA: Brooks/Cole.

Campbell, C. (1986). *Managing the Presidency: Carter, Reagan and the Search for Executive Harmony*. Pittsburgh: University of Pittsburgh Press.

Care of Institutionalized Mentally Disabled Persons: Joint Hearings Before the Subcommittee on the Handicapped of the Senate Committee on Labor and Human Resources and the Subcommittee on Labor, Health and Human Services, Education and Related Agencies Appropriations of the Senate Committee on Appropriations, Parts 1 and 2, 99th Cong., 1st Sess. (1985).

Civil Rights Act of 1960, Title VI, 42 U.S.C. Section 1971(c) (1981).

Civil Rights Act of 1964, Titles II and VII, 42 U.S.C. Sections 2000a-5, 2000b, 2000c-6, 2000e-6 (1981).

Civil Rights Act of 1968, Title VIII, 42 U.S.C. Section 3613 (1994 Supp.).

Civil Rights of Institutionalized Persons Act, 42 U.S.C. Section 1997 (1981).

Civil rights of institutionalized persons act. (1983). *Mental Disability Law Reporter*, 7, 5–8.

Civil Rights of Institutionalized Persons Act: Hearings Before the Subcommittee on Courts, Civil Liberties, and the Administration of Justice and the Subcommittee on Civil and Constitutional Rights of the House Committee on the Judiciary, 98th Cong., 1st Sess. (1983).

Civil Rights of Institutionalized Persons Act: Hearings Before the Subcommittee on Courts, Civil Liberties, and the Administration of Justice and the Subcommittee on Civil and Constitutional Rights of the House Committee on the Judiciary, 98th Cong., 2d Sess. (1984).

Civil Rights of the Institutionalized: Hearings on S.10 Before the Subcommittee on the Constitution of the Senate Committee on the Judiciary, 96th Cong., 1st Sess. (1979).

Clayton, C. W. (1992). *The Politics of Justice: The Attorney General and the Making of Legal Policy*. Armonk, NY: M. E. Sharpe.

Confirmation Hearings on Federal Appointments, Part 2: Hearing Before the Senate Judiciary Committee, 98th Cong., 1st Sess. (1983).

Confirmation Hearings on Federal Appointments, Part 3: Hearing Before the Senate Judiciary Committee, 98th Cong., 2d Sess. (1984).

Confirmation Hearings on Federal Appointments, Part 2: Hearing Before the Senate Judiciary Committee, 99th Cong., 1st Sess. (1985).

126 Cong. Rec. S1712–13 (daily ed. Feb. 26, 1980).

Cook, T. M. (1983, October 18). Resignation from the Department of Justice: Unpublished Memorandum to W. F. Smith (on file with Karen Holt).

Cooper, Charles J. Interview with author. Washington, DC, 2 September 1993.

Cornwell, J. K. (1988). CRIPA: The failure of federal intervention for mentally retarded people. *Yale Law Journal*, 97, 845–862.

Davis v. Henderson, C.A. 77–423 (M.D. La. 1982).

Departments of Commerce, Justice, and State, the Judiciary, and Related Agencies Appropriations for 1981. Part 6: Department of Justice: Hearings Before the Subcommittee on Commerce, Justice, State, and the Judiciary Appropriations of the House Committee on Appropriations, 96th Cong., 2d Sess. (1980).

Departments of Commerce, Justice, and State, the Judiciary, and Related Agencies Appropriations for 1982. Part 7: Department of Justice: Hearings Before the Subcommittee on Commerce, Justice, State, and the Judiciary Appropriations of the House Committee on Appropriations, 97th Cong., 1st Sess. (1981).

_____. *Appropriations for 1983. Part 7: Department of Justice: Hearings Before the Subcommittee on Commerce, Justice, State, and the Judiciary Appropriations of the House Committee on Appropriations*, 97th Cong., 2d Sess. (1982).

_____ . *Appropriations for 1984. Part 6: Department of Justice: Hearings Before the Subcommittee on Commerce, Justice, State, and the Judiciary Appropriations of the House Committee on Appropriations*, 98th Cong., 1st Sess. (1983).

_____ . *Appropriations for 1985. Part 8: Department of Justice: Hearings Before the Subcommittee on Commerce, Justice, State, and the Judiciary Appropriations of the House Committee on Appropriations*, 98th Cong., 2d Sess. (1984).

_____ . *Appropriations for 1986. Part 7: Department of Justice: Hearings Before the Subcommittee on Commerce, Justice, State, and the Judiciary Appropriations of the House Committee on Appropriations*, 99th Cong., 1st Sess. (1985).

_____ . *Appropriations for 1987. Part 4: Department of Justice: Hearings Before the Subcommittee on Commerce, Justice, State, and the Judiciary Appropriations of the House Committee on Appropriations*, 99th Cong., 2d Sess. (1986).

_____ . *Appropriations for 1988. Part 4: Department of Justice: Hearings Before the Subcommittee on Commerce, Justice, State, and the Judiciary Appropriations of the House Committee on Appropriations*, 100th Cong., 1st Sess. (1987).

_____ . *Appropriations for 1989. Part 6: Department of Justice: Hearings Before the Subcommittee on Commerce, Justice, State, and the Judiciary Appropriations of the House Committee on Appropriations*, 100th Cong., 2d Sess. (1988).

Department of Justice Authorization for FY 1983: Hearing Before the House Committee on the Judiciary, 97th Cong., 2d Sess. (1982).

Department of Justice Authorization for FY 1989 (Civil, Criminal and Civil Rights Divisions), Part 2: Hearings Before the Senate Committee on the Judiciary, 100th Cong., 2d Sess. (1988).

Department of Justice Confirmations, Part 2: Hearings Before the Senate Judiciary Committee, 97th Cong., 1st Sess. (1981).

Detlefsen, R. R. (1991). *Civil Rights Under Reagan*. San Francisco: Institute for Contemporary Studies.

Devine, D. J. (1987). Political administration: The right way. In R. Rector & M. Sanera (Eds.), *Steering the Elephant: How Washington Works* (pp. 125–135). New York: Universe Books.

Dinerstein, R. (1984). The absence of justice. *Nebraska Law Review, 63*, 680–708.

_____ . (1989). Rights of institutionalized disabled persons. In W. L. Taylor & R. C. Govan (Eds.), *One Nation Indivisible: The Civil Rights Challenge for the 1990's* (pp. 388–413). Washington, DC: Citizens' Commission on Civil Rights.

Dolan, M. W. (1993). Political influence on the Department of Justice: Are the pressures only external? *Journal of Law and Politics, 9*, 309–315.

Downs, A. (1967). *Inside Bureaucracy*. Boston: Little, Brown.

Durant, R. F. (1987). Toward assessing the administrative presidency: Public lands, the BLM, and the Reagan administration. *Public Administration Review, 47*, 180–189.

_____ . (1990). Beyond fear or favor: Appointee-careerist relations in the post-Reagan era. *Public Administration Review, 50*, 319–331.

_____ . (1992). *The Administrative Presidency Revisited: Public Lands, the BLM, and the Reagan Revolution.* Albany: SUNY Press.

Eads, G. C., & Fix, M. (1982). Regulatory policy. In J. L. Palmer & I. V. Sawhill (Eds.). *The Reagan Experiment: An Examination of Economic and Social Policies Under the Reagan Administration* (pp. 129–153). Washington, DC: Urban Institute Press.

Eastland, T. (1988). Reagan justice: Combating excess, strengthening the rule of law. *Policy Review, 46,* 16–23.

_____ . (1992). *Energy in the Executive.* New York: Free Press.

Edwards, G. C. III. (1980). *Implementing Public Policy.* Washington, DC: Congressional Quarterly.

Enforcement of Section 504 of the Rehabilitation Act: Institutional Care and Services for Retarded Citizens: Hearing Before the Subcommittee on the Handicapped of the Senate Committee on Labor and Human Resources, 98th Cong., 1st Sess. (1983).

Erickson, P. D. (1985). *Reagan Speaks: The Making of an American Myth.* New York: New York University Press.

42 U.S.C. Section 1983 (1981).

Gates v. Collier, C.A. 73–1790 (N.D. Miss., August 13, 1981).

Gentry, M. (1981). The Reagan corrections program: Less money, more states' rights. *Corrections Magazine, 7,* 29–36.

Golden, M. M. (1992). Exit, voice, loyalty, and neglect: Bureaucratic responses to presidential control. *Journal of Public Administration Research and Theory, 2,* 29–62.

Goldstein, M. L. (1992). *America's Hollow Government: How Washington Has Failed the People.* Homewood, IL: Business One Irwin.

Gordon, D. (1986). Civil wrongs and the handicapped. *Justice Watch, 6,* 1–3, 6–7.

Greenstein, F. (1983). The need for an early appraisal of the Reagan presidency. In F. Greenstein (Ed.), *The Reagan Presidency: An Early Assessment* (pp. 1–20). Baltimore: Johns Hopkins University Press.

Halderman v. Pennhurst State School and Hospital, 446 F. Supp. 1295 (E.D. Pa. 1977).

Heatherly, C. L. (Ed.). (1981). *Mandate for Leadership: Policy Management in a Conservative Administration.* Washington, DC: Heritage Foundation.

Heclo, H. (1975, Winter). OMB and the presidency—the problem of neutral competence. *The Public Interest,* 80–82.

_____ . (1977). *A Government of Strangers: Executive Politics in Washington.* Washington, DC: Brookings Institution.

_____ . (1983). One executive branch or many? In A. King (Ed.), *Both Ends of the Avenue: The Presidency, the Executive Branch, and Congress in the 1980's* (pp. 26–58). Washington, DC: American Enterprise Institute for Public Policy Research.

_____ . (1984). An executive's success can have costs. In L. M. Salamon & M.S. Lund (Eds.), *The Reagan Presidency and the Governing of America* (pp. 371–374). Washington, DC: Urban Institute Press.

_____ . (1987). The in- and- outer system: A critical assessment. *Political Science Quarterly, 103,* 37–45.

Henderson, P. G. (1988). *Managing the Presidency: The Eisenhower Legacy—From Kennedy to Reagan.* Boulder: Westview Press.

Heritage Foundation. (1984). *Mandate for Leadership II: Continuing the Conservative Revolution.* Washington, DC: The Foundation.

Hill, J. S., & Brazier, J. E. (1991). Constraining administrative decisions: A critical examination of the structure and process hypothesis. *Journal of Law, Economics, and Organization, 7,* 373–400.

H.R. 9400, 95th Cong., 1st Sess. (1977).

H.R. 3033, 100th Cong., 1st Sess. (1987).

H.R. Rep. No. 897, 96th Cong., 2d Sess. (1980) (conference report), reprinted in 1980 U.S.C.C.A.N. 832–842.

Hirschman, A. O. (1970). *Exit, Voice, and Loyalty: Responses to Decline in Firms, Organizations, and States.* Cambridge, MA: Harvard University Press.

Huddleston, M. W. (1987). Background paper. In The Twentieth Century Fund Task Force on the Senior Executive Service, *The Government's Managers* (pp. 25–88). New York: Priority.

Hunter, L. (pseudonym) (1987). Turning the iron triangle upside down: Alfred Regnery and juvenile justice. In R. Rector & M. Sanera (Eds.), *Steering the Elephant: How Washington Works* (pp. 294–315). New York: Universe Books.

Huntley, Lynn Walker. Interview with author (telephone). New York, 2 February 1995.

Ingraham, P. W. (1987). Policy implementation and the public service. In R. B. Denhardt and E. T. Jennings, Jr. (eds.), *The Revitalization of the Public Service* (pp. 145–155). Columbia, MO: University of Missouri Press.

Ingraham, P. W. (1991). Political direction and policy change in three federal departments. In J. P. Pfiffner (Ed.), *The Managerial Presidency* (pp. 180–193). Pacific Grove, CA: Brooks/Cole.

Ingraham, P. W., & Ban, C. (1988). Politics and merit: Can they meet in a public service model? *Review of Public Personnel Administration, 8,* 7–19.

Jackson v. Indiana, 406 U.S. 715 (1972).

Kaufman, H. (1956). Emerging conflicts in the doctrines of public administration. *American Political Science Review, 50,* 1057–1073.

Killenbeck, M. R. (1986). We have met the imbeciles and they are us: The courts and citizens with mental retardation. *Nebraska Law Review, 65,* 768–807.

Kirschten, D. (1983, April 9). Administration using Carter-era reform to manipulate the layers of government. *National Journal,* 732–736.

Kmiec, D. E. (1992). *The Attorney General's Lawyer: Inside the Meese Justice Department*. New York: Praeger.

Kraft, M. E., & Vig, N. J. (1984). Environmental policy in the Reagan presidency. *Political Science Quarterly, 99*, 415–439.

Kristol, W. (1985). Can-do government. *Policy Review, 31*, 62–66.

Landsberg, B. K. (1993). The role of civil service attorneys and political appointees in making policy in the Civil Rights Division of the United States Department of Justice. *Journal of Law and Politics, 9*, 275–289.

Leadership Conference on Civil Rights. (1983). Without justice: A report on the conduct of the Justice Department in civil rights in 1981–82. *Black Law Journal, 8*, 29–59.

Light, P. C. (1987). When worlds collide: The political and career nexus. In G. C. Mackenzie (Ed.), *The In- and- Outers: Presidential Appointees and Transient Government in Washington* (pp. 156–173). Baltimore: Johns Hopkins University Press.

Lowery, D., & Rusbelt, C. E. (1986). Bureaucratic responses to antibureaucratic administrations: Federal employee reaction to the Reagan election. *Administration and Society, 18*, 45–75.

Lynn, L. E., Jr. (1984). The Reagan administration and the renitent bureaucracy. In L. M. Salamon & M. S. Lund (Eds.). *The Reagan Presidency and the Governing of America* (pp. 340–370). Washington, DC: Urban Institute Press.

MacCoon, John P. Interview with author. Chattanooga, TN, 20 April 1994.

Mann, T. E. (1990). Thinking about the Reagan presidency. In L. Berman (Ed.), *Looking Back on the Reagan Presidency* (pp. 18–29). Baltimore: Johns Hopkins University Press.

Maranto, R. (1993). *Politics and Bureaucracy in the Modern Presidency: Careerists and Appointees in the Reagan Administration*. Westport, CT: Greenwood Press.

Menzel, D. C. (1983). Redirecting the implementation of a law: The Reagan administration and coal surface mining regulation. *Public Administration Review, 43*, 411–420.

Mezey, M. L. (1989). *Congress, the President, and Public Policy*. Boulder, CO: Westview Press.

Moe, T. M. (1985). The politicized presidency. In J. E. Chubb & P. E. Peterson (Eds.), *The New Direction in American Politics* (pp. 235–271). Washington, DC: Brookings Institution.

Nathan, R. P. (1983a). *The Administrative Presidency*. New York: John Wiley.

_____ . (1983b). The Reagan presidency in domestic affairs. In F. Greenstein (Ed.), *The Reagan Presidency: An Early Assessment* (pp. 49–81). Baltimore: Johns Hopkins University Press.

_____ . (1984). Political administration is legitimate. In L. M. Salamon & M. S. Lund (Eds.), *The Reagan Presidency and the Governing of America* (pp. 375–379). Washington, DC: Urban Institute Press.

_____ . (1986). Institutional change under Reagan. In J. L. Palmer (Ed.), *Perspectives on the Reagan Years* (pp. 121–145). Washington, DC: Urban Institute Press.

Neustadt, R. (1980). *Presidential Power: The Politics of Leadership from FDR to Carter*. New York: John Wiley.

_____ . (1990). *Presidential Power and the Modern Presidents: The Politics of Leadership from Roosevelt to Reagan*. New York: Free Press.

Newland, C. A. (1983). A mid-term appraisal—The Reagan Presidency: Limited government and political administration. *Public Administration Review, 43*, 1–21.

New York State Association for Retarded Children v. Rockefeller, 357 F. Supp. 752 (E.D.N.Y. 1975).

Niskanen, W., Jr. (1987). Lessons for political appointees. In R. Rector & M. Sanera (Eds.), *Steering the Elephant: How Washington Works* (pp. 57–61). New York: Universe Books.

Nomination of William Bradford Reynolds to be Associate Attorney General of the U.S.: Hearings Before the Senate Committee on the Judiciary, 99th Cong., 1st Sess. (1985).

Office of Management and Budget. (1983). *Budget of the United States: Special Analyses*.

Oversight Hearings on Title I: Child Abuse Prevention and Treatment and Adoption Reform Act of 1978: Hearings Before the Subcommittee on Select Education of the House Committee on Education and Labor, 96th Cong., 2d Sess. (1980).

Palumbo, D. J., & Calista, D. J. (1990). Opening up the black box: Implementation and the policy process. In D. J. Palumbo & D. J. Calista (Eds.), *Implementation and the Policy Process: Opening Up the Black Box* (pp. 3–17). Westport, CT: Greenwood Press.

Peabody, A. E. (1982, August 4). Unpublished memorandum to J. Harvie Wilkinson. Appendix N, Cook, T. M. (1983, October 18). Resignation from the Department of Justice: Unpublished Memorandum to W. F. Smith (on file with Karen Holt).

Peabody, Arthur E. Jr. Interview with author. Washington, DC, 23 March 1994.

Percy, S. L. (1989). *Disability, Civil Rights, and Public Policy: The Politics of Implementation*. Tuscaloosa, AL: University of Alabama Press.

Pfiffner, J. P. (1988). *The Strategic Presidency: Hitting the Ground Running*. Chicago: Dorsey Press.

_____ . (1991). Political appointees and career executives: The democracy-bureaucracy nexus. In J. P. Pfiffner (Ed.), *The Managerial Presidency* (pp. 167–179). Pacific Grove, CA: Brooks/Cole.

Plotkin, R. (1981, August 2). Injustice department. *New York Times*, p. A15.

Plotkin, R., Davison, P., & Kaufman, J. (1989). Civil rights enforcement policies with respect to prisoners' rights. In W. L. Taylor & R. C. Govan (Eds.), *One Nation Indivisible: The Civil Rights Challenge for the 1990's* (pp. 414–430). Washington, DC: Citizens' Commission on Civil Rights.

Plotkin, Robert. Interview with author. Washington, DC, 1 September 1993.

President's Committee on Mental Retardation. (1984, June 11). The rights of mentally retarded citizens. Cong. Rec. S15621.

Radin, B. A. (1977). *Implementation, Change, and the Federal Bureaucracy: School Desegregation Policy in HEW 1964–1968.* New York: Teachers College Press.

Rector, R., & Sanera, M. (1987). The Reagan presidency and policy change. In R. Rector & M. Sanera (Eds.), *Steering the Elephant: How Washington Works* (pp. 328–349). New York: Universe Books.

Rehabilitation Act of 1973, 29 U.S.C. Section 794 (1994 Supp.).

Rein, M., & Rabinovitz, F. (1978). Implementation: A theoretical perspective. In W. D. Burnham & M.W. Weinberg (Eds.), *American Politics and Public Policy* (pp. 307–335). Cambridge, MA: MIT Press.

The Reynolds Nomination. (1985, June 4). *The Washington Post*, p. A16.

Reynolds, W. B. (1982, June 24). Constitutional rights of institutionalized persons: Memorandum to Arthur E. Peabody, Jr. Appendix M to T. M. Cook, Resignation from the Department of Justice: Unpublished Memorandum to W. F. Smith (1983, October 18) (on file with Karen Holt).

———. (1983, January 17). Letter to Norman S. Rosenberg, Director, Mental Health Law Project (on file with Karen Holt).

———. (1983, April 20). Memorandum to Timothy M. Cook. Appendix A to T. M. Cook, Resignation from the Department of Justice: Unpublished Memorandum to W. F. Smith (1983, October 18) (on file with Karen Holt).

———. (1983, November 16). Memorandum to Thomas P. DeCair (on file with Karen Holt).

———. (1984a). A defense of the Reagan administration's civil rights policies: An interview with Assistant Attorney General William Bradford Reynolds. *New Perspectives, 16*(3), 34–38.

———. (1984b). The "civil rights establishment" is all wrong. *Human Rights, 12*(1), 34–41.

———. (1986). The Reagan administration and civil rights: Winning the war against discrimination. *University of Illinois Law Review, 1986,* 1001–1023.

———. (1989). The Reagan administration's civil rights policy: The challenge for the future. *Vanderbilt Law Review, 42,* 993–1001.

Reynolds, William Bradford. Interview with author, Washington, DC, 2 September 1993.

Rockman, B. A. (1993). Tightening the reins: The federal executive and the management philosophy of the Reagan presidency. *Presidential Studies Quarterly, 23,* 103–114.

Rourke, F. E. (1992). Responsiveness and neutral competence in American bureaucracy. *Public Administration Review, 52,* 539–546.

Ruiz v. Estelle, 679 F.2d 1115 (5th Cir. 1982).

Sabatier, P., & Zafonte, M. (1994). *Are bureaucrats and scientists neutral? Two models applied to San Francisco Bay/Delta Water Policy.* Paper presented at the annual meeting of the International Political Science Association, Berlin, Germany.

Sanera, M. (1984). Implementing the mandate. In Heritage Foundation, *Mandate for Leadership II: Continuing the Conservative Revolution* (pp. 459–559). Washington, DC: Heritage Foundation.

Santana v. Collazo, C.A. 75–1187 (D.P.R. Sept. 11, 1980).

Schick, A. (1983). Politics through law: Congressional limitations on executive discretion. In A. King (Ed.), *Both Ends of the Avenue: The Presidency, the Executive Branch, and Congress in the 1980's* (pp. 154–184). Washington, DC: American Enterprise Institute for Public Policy Research.

Schmidt, R. E., & Abramson, M. A. (1983). Politics and performance: What does it mean for civil servants? *Public Administration Review, 43*, 155–160.

Schoen, Benjamin. Interview with author. Washington, DC, 23 March 1994.

Selig, J. L. (1986). The Reagan Justice Department and civil rights: What went wrong. *University of Illinois Law Review, 1985*, 785–835.

S. Rep. No. 416, 96th Cong., 1st Sess. (1979), reprinted in 1980 U.S.C.C.A.N. 787–832.

S. 1393, 95th Cong., 2d Sess. (1978).

S. 10, 96th Cong., 1st Sess. (1979).

S. 1540, 100th Cong., 1st Sess. (1987).

Shanley, R. A. (1992). *Presidential Influence and Environmental Policy*. Westport, CT: Greenwood Press.

Shull, S. A. (1989). *The President and Civil Rights Policy: Leadership and Change*. Westport, CT: Greenwood Press.

_____. (1993). *A Kinder, Gentler Racism? The Reagan-Bush Civil Rights Legacy*. New York: M. E. Sharpe.

Shull, S. A. & Ringelstein, A. C. (1989). Presidential attention, support, and symbolism in civil rights. *Social Science Journal, 26*, 45–54.

Smith, W. F. (1991). *Law and Justice in the Reagan Administration*. Stanford: Hoover Institution Press.

Spangler, S. E. (1982). Snatching legislative power: The Justice Department's refusal to enforce the parental kidnapping prevention act. *Journal of Criminal Law and Criminology, 73*, 1176–1203.

Stanfield, R. L. (1983, May 28). Reagan courting women, minorities, but it may be too late to win them. *National Journal*, pp. 1118–1123.

State and Local Fiscal Assistance Act of 1972, P.L. 92–512, 92d Congress, 2d Sess. (1972).

Taylor, S., Jr. (1984, June 22). When goals of boss and his staff lawyers clash. *New York Times*, p. A14.

Thornton, M. (1982, September 29). New policy on mental patient rights upsets lawyers, health community. *Washington Post*, p. A2.

U.S. Department of Justice, Civil Rights Division (1982–1990). *Reports of the Attorney General to the Congress of the United States on the Administration of the*

Civil Rights of Institutionalized Persons Act for Fiscal Years 1981–1989. Washington, DC: U.S. Department of Justice.

U. S. Department of Justice, Office of the Attorney General (1975). *Annual Report of the Attorney General of the United States 1974.* Washington, DC: U.S. Government Printing Office.

_____. (1979). *Annual Report of the Attorney General of the United States 1978.* Washington, DC: U.S. Government Printing Office.

_____. (1981). *Annual Report of the Attorney General of the United States 1980.* Washington, DC: U.S. Government Printing Office.

U. S. Department of Justice, Office of the Attorney General, Office of Inmate Grievance Procedure (1981, January 16). Certification standards for inmate grievance procedures. *Federal Register, 46,* pp. 3843–3852.

_____. Office of Inmate Grievance Procedure (1981, July 16). Certification standards for inmate grievance procedures. *Federal Register, 46,* pp. 36865–36869.

U. S. Department of Justice, Office of the Attorney General (1982–1989). *Annual Reports of the Attorney General of the United States 1981–1988.* Washington, DC: U.S. Government Printing Office.

United States v. Connecticut, No. N-86–252 (D. Conn. July 25, 1986).

United States v. Indiana, No. IP 84 411C (S.D. Ind. April 6, 1984).

United States v. Massachusetts, No. 85–0632–MA (D. Mass. August 25, 1987).

United States v. Mattson, 600 F.2d 1295 (9th Cir. 1979).

United States v. Michigan, 680 F. Supp. 928 (W.D. Mich. 1987).

United States v. Oregon, No. 86–961–LE (D. Or. July 28, 1986).

United States v. Solomon, 419 F. Supp. 358 (D. Md. 1976), *aff'd,* 563 F.2d 1121 (4th Cir. 1977).

The Washington Council of Lawyers (1983). Reagan civil rights: The first twenty months. *New York Law School Human Rights Annual, 1,* 117–171.

Waterman, R. W. (1989). *Presidential Influence and the Administrative State.* Knoxville, TN: University of Tennessee Press.

West, W. F., & Cooper, J. (1985). The rise of administrative clearance. In G. C. Edwards III, S. A. Shull, & N. C. Thomas. (Eds.), *The Presidency and Public Policymaking* (pp. 192–214). Pittsburgh: University of Pittsburgh Press.

Whinston, S. A. (1983, April 12). Memorandum to Arthur E. Peabody (on file with Karen Holt).

Williams, J. (1985, June 4). Reynolds sets defense on Justice nomination. *Washington Post,* p. A5.

Wines, M. (1982, March 27). Administration says it merely seeks a "better way" to enforce civil rights. *National Journal,* pp. 536–541.

_____. (1982, November 20). The wheels of justice—choose your version. *National Journal,* p. 1998.

Withey, M., & Cooper, W. (1989). Predicting exit, voice, loyalty and neglect. *Administrative Science Quarterly, 34,* 60–62.

Wolfson, A. (1986). The new McCarthyism: William Bradford Reynolds and the politics of character assassination. *Policy Review, 35*, 60–62.

Wood, B. D., & Waterman, R. W. (1991). The dynamics of political control of the bureaucracy. *American Political Science Review, 85*, 801–828.

Wood, B. D., West, W. F., & Bohte, J. (1993). *The politics of administrative design: Legislative coalitions, political uncertainty, and the bureaucracy.* Paper presented at the annual meeting of the American Political Science Association, Washington, DC.

Wyatt v. Stickney, 325 F. Supp. 781 (M.D. Ala. 1971), 334 F. Supp. 1341 (M.D. Ala. 1971), 344 F. Supp. 387 (M.D. Ala. 1972), *aff'd sub nom., Wyatt v. Aderholt*, 503 F.2d 1305 (5th Cir. 1974).

Youngberg v. Romeo, 457 U.S. 307 (1982).

Index

ACLU, 50, 74, 76–77

Administrative presidency strategy: criticism, 3–5; definition, 1, 4; factors influencing success, 7, 10, 123–24; success, 10, 107, 118, 120–21, 124

Alabama mental institutions, 14

American Bar Association Commission on the Mentally Disabled, 75

American Psychological Association, 76

Amicus curiae: Department of Justice participation, 14, 34, 39–40, 95; participation by others, 77–78

Apoliticals, 100

Assenting loyalists, 100

Atascadero State Hospital, 46

Attorney General, statutory authority, 14–16, 18–19

Attorney General's Honors Program, 57

Aversive treatment, 76

"Baby Doe" cases, 48

Battle v. Anderson, 14

Bayh, Birch, 17–18

Beard, Hugh "Joe," 56

Bell, Griffin, 18

Biloxi, Mississippi jail, 40–41, 112

Biden, Joseph, 68, 70

Blackmun, Harry, 43

Bolton, John, 72

Bureau of Land Management, 5

Bureau of Prisons, 34, 109

Burger, Warren, 43

Busing, 28, 68, 70, 82

Calista, Donald, 3, 26

Careerists, generally: administration view of, 25; morale, 7–9; role, 26; turnover, 24

Carter, Jimmy, 2, 25, 92, 108; Administration, civil rights policy, 28; Administration, CRIPA enforcement, 2, 33, 35–36, 53, 112

Civil Rights Act of 1960, 16

Civil Rights Act of 1964, 16–17

Civil Rights Act of 1968, 16–17

Civil Rights of Institutionalized Persons Act (CRIPA); 15–16, 18; enforcement policy of Reagan Administration, 3, 28, 30, 43; initiating investigations, 40, 107; law-

About the Author

KAREN E. HOLT is Director of the Office of Equal Opportunity Programs at the University of Virginia. In 1985, she left the Department of Justice in Washington to join the General Counsel's Office of the University of Tennessee. While there, she obtained her Ph.D. in Political Science. Dr. Holt continues her active practice of law, concentrating in employment and discrimination litigation.

ISBN 0-275-95997-X

90000>

EAN

9 780275 959975

HARDCOVER BAR CODE